Get the Money In the Door

Physician Billing Basics

SARAH J. HOLT, PhD, FACMPE

Medical Group Management Association
104 Inverness Terrace East
Englewood, CO 80112-5306
877.275.6462
mgma.com

Production Credits
Publisher: Marilee E. Aust
Project Editor: Anne Serrano, MA
Copy Editor: Katharine Dvorak
Composition: Jacquie Wallace
Proofreader: Mary Kay Kozyra
Indexer: Lucie Haskins
Cover Design: Ian Serff, Serff Creative Group, Inc.

Library of Congress Cataloging-in-Publication Data

Holt, Sarah J.
   Get the money in the door: physician billing basics/Sarah J. Holt
      p.; cm.
   Includes bibliography references and index.
   Summary: "An insurance primer and personal handbook for insurance staff, a teaching and hiring tool for managers with direct responsibility for insurance departments, and a resource for medical practice executives who need to be aware of what insurance department employees must know to maximize their role in the revenue cycle"—Provided by publisher.
   ISBN 978-1-56829-340-0
   1. Medical fees. 2. Health insurance claims. 3. Medicine–Practice–Finance. 4. Medicine–Practice–Accounting. I. Medical Group Management Association. II. Title.
   [DNLM: 1. Financial Management–organization & administration–United States. 2. Practice Management, Medical–organization & administration–United States. 3. Insurance Claim Reporting–United States. 4. Insurance, Health, Reimbursement–United States. W 80 H758g 2010]
   R728.5.H65 2010
   610.68'1–dc22
                         2009016061

Item #9001
ISBN: 978-1-56829-340-0

Printed in the United States of America
10 9 8 7 6 5 4 3 2 1

This book is dedicated to my daughters, Takara Stanley and Rachel Stanley,
who have always inspired me to do more than I could have ever have done without
them and to my husband, Dennis, who has always believed in my ability.
I have received additional support from many others — first, the surgeons of
Cape Girardeau Surgical Clinic, my employers. They have given me the freedom and
encouragement to grow as a professional. Second, I wish to acknowledge my colleagues
at MGMA and ACMPE from whom I always learn and who motivate me to seek
continuous improvement as a professional. Lastly, I want to acknowledge my own
medical office insurance staff members as well as all medical office insurance
staff members who do nearly impossible work with little recognition.
To all I thank you.

Contents

Introduction xi

Chapter 1 ▪ **Understanding Health Care Insurance** 1

   Government Insurance 1

      Medicare 2

         Medicare Parts A, B, C, and D 2

         Actors in Medicare Claims Processing 3

         Coverage Eligibility 4

         Medicare Participation 5

         Site-of-Service Payment Consideration 5

         Fee-for-Service Plans 5

         Managed Care Plans 6

         Payment Requests 6

         Advanced Beneficiary Notice 6

         Non-Participating Providers 6

         Primary and Secondary Payers 7

         National Correct Coding Initiative 7

         Enrollment in the Medicare Program — Providers 7

         Enrollment in the Medicare Program — Beneficiaries 7

         Medicare Website 8

      Medicaid 8

         Medicaid Eligibility Groups 9

         Eligibility Time Frame 10

         Mandatory Services 10

      TRICARE 10

   Commercial For-Profit Insurance 11

Exhibit 1.1 Major Categories of Commercial Insurance

Fee-for-Service Plans 12

Managed Care Plans 13

    Exhibit 1.2 Fundamental Elements of Health Insurance

Health Maintenance Organizations 15

Preferred Provider Organizations 15

Point-of-Service Plans 15

    Exhibit 1.3 Self-Insured Plans Benefits Comparison

COBRA 17

Workers' Compensation 18

Direct Contracting 18

Non-Governmental Not-for-Profit Insurance 19

Original Blue Cross Blue Shield 19

Private Not-for-Profits.. 20

Chapter 2 ▪ Understanding Medical Office Insurance Staff 21

Medical Office Insurance Staff Act as Street-Level Bureaucrats 21

Information Processing by Medical Office Insurance Staff 23

Key Challenges for Medical Office Insurance Staff 24

Adhering to External Regulation 24

Coping with Information Overload............................ 26

Managing Frustration 27

Resulting Characteristics of Medical Office Insurance Staff 28

Responsible 28

Persistent 29

Self-Reliant 30

Place Emphasis on Experience 31

Effective Communicators..................................... 32

Major Tensions Confronted by Medical Office Insurance Staff 33

Perceptions of Medical Office Insurance Staff Members 33

Attitudes of Medical Office Insurance Staff Members 34

Beliefs of Medical Office Insurance Staff Members.............. 35

Actions of Medical Office Insurance Staff Members 36

Tension between Independent and Dependent Behavior 36

Tension between Patient and Organizational Needs 37

Influences in Medicare Implementation 40

Decision Making... 40

Service Delivery... 41

Medical Office Insurance Staff: An Emerging Profession 42

Chapter 3 ■ **Elements of Billing and Payment** 45

    Current Procedural Terminology 45

    International Classification of Diseases, Ninth Revision 46

    Relative Value Unit 47

    The Correct Coding Initiative 48

        Exhibit 3.1 CCI Edits Tables

    Patient Paperwork 52

        Insurance Cards 53

        Patient Identification 53

        Signature on File 53

    Insurance Verification 54

    Role of HIPAA 57

    Compliance 58

    Claims Format 59

Chapter 4 ■ **Importance of Insurance in the Revenue Cycle** 63

    Elements of the Revenue Cycle 63

        Contracting 63

        Information Collection 64

        Charge Capture 65

        Charge Entry 66

        Generating and Submitting Claims 66

        Working Claims 67

    Explanation of Benefits 68

        Reading EOBs 68

        Interpreting EOBs 69

        Participation 69

        Non-Participation 70

    Physician Credentialing 70

        Exhibit 4.1 Physician Credentialing Checklist

    Documentation and Coding 74

        E/M History 75

        E/M Examination 76

        Medical Decision Making 76

    Fraud and Abuse 77

        Fraud 77

        Abuse 78

    Filing Claims 78

        Clearinghouses 78

        Timely Filing 79

        Exhibit 4.2 Medicare Timely Filing Table

        Accuracy 80

Payment Posting 81

Account Follow-Up 82

Prioritizing Work 82

Rejections and Denials 83

Appeals 84

Medicare Appeals Process 84

Reopening a Claim 85

Correspondence 86

Insurance Carriers 86

Patients 86

Collections 87

Credit Balances 87

Offsets 88

Chapter 5 ▪ Scenarios 89

Scenario 1 89

Scenario 2 90

Scenario 3 90

Scenario 4 91

Scenario 5 92

Scenario 6 92

Scenario 7 93

Scenario 8 93

Scenario 9 94

Scenario 10 94

Scenario 11 95

Scenario 12 95

Scenario 13 96

Scenario 14 96

Scenario 15 97

Scenario 16 97

Scenario 17 98

Scenario 18 98

Scenario 19 99

Scenario 20 99

Scenario 21 100

Scenario 22 100

Scenario 23 101

Scenario 24 101

Scenario 25 102

Appendix A ■ **Modifiers** 103

Appendix B ■ **Place of Service Codes** 107

Glossary 109
About the Author 129
Index 131

Introduction

Medical office insurance staff members play a critical role in a medical practice. They understand — perhaps more than anyone — that their role is to "get the money in the door." Yet, it is typical that the only training insurance staff members receive is on the job, and that this training is solely dependent on what the trainer knows and how well he or she conveys the information to these adult learners. Individuals are hired because they have had insurance experience in another organization, or they are moved from somewhere else in the medical practice to fill a need in the insurance department. Neither hiring track ensures that these employees will succeed. This book seeks to change that dynamic.

Get the Money In the Door serves as an insurance primer and personal handbook for insurance staff members, a teaching and hiring tool for managers with direct responsibility for insurance departments, and as a resource for medical practice executives who need to be aware of what insurance department employees must know to maximize their role in the revenue cycle.

The book helps break down the divide between managers who are highly dependent on the work of their insurance department staff to bring in revenue, but are too often separated from the staff members who act with discretion and autonomy.

The first four chapters illuminate the reader about health care insurance in the medical practice. Chapter 1 lays out a framework for understanding health care insurance in the United States. It outlines three major types of insurance — governmental (including Medicare, Medicaid, and TRICARE), commercial, and non-governmental not-for-profit.

The contents of Chapter 2, based on qualitative research studying medical office insurance staff, provide insight into how medical office insurance staff members perform their complex tasks, the situations they face, and the coping strategies they develop to deal with the stress and how their perceptions, attitudes, and beliefs impact service delivery.

There is a lot of uncertainty that exists due to the complex and confusing sets of regulations involved in medical insurance reimbursement. Chapter 3 addresses all aspects of billing and payments to alleviate some of the uncertainty. This chapter also reviews the items that determine the charge value of services and procedures to lessen the ambiguity for medical office insurance staff.

Chapter 4 deals specifically with the importance of the revenue cycle. Although medical office insurance staff members play a critical role in the revenue cycle in medical practices, they are rarely exposed to the entire breadth of the revenue cycle as well as lack information about where their role fits into the process as a whole. This chapter makes them aware of the various elements of the revenue cycle and gives them a better understanding of the importance of their role in the medical practice.

Chapter 5 is a tool consisting of 25 scenarios. Each scenario describes a real-life situation that medical insurance staff deal with every day and four possible options of how to handle it. The reader is asked to choose which possibility he or she feels is the best, then feedback is provided as to which choice actually would be the preferred choice. These problem-solving exercises teach participants to define problems correctly, look at alternatives to resolve situations, and choose the best alternative. These scenarios provide an opportunity for managers to use as a hiring tool to assess medical insurance knowledge and as a teaching tool for existing insurance staff.

Because medical office insurance staff members process such a high volume of information that is similar overall but very different in the particulars, they suffer from information overload. These individuals often need clarification or confirmation when working with an acronym or a term. Additionally, because these staff members have often been trained on the job by peers, some information may have been conveyed incorrectly, and these individuals continue to function based on misinformation. To aid medical office insurance staff members in being more productive, a glossary of terms for daily use specifically for them is provided at the end of this book.

CHAPTER ONE

Understanding Health Care Insurance

Most health care reimbursement occurs through a complex process of filing and following up on health care insurance claims. "Reimbursement for health care services is one of the most complex processes of the health care system."[1] Undoubtedly, the work of insurance staff can be a daunting task. The health insurance body of knowledge is so large that it is difficult for one person to master it in total. Individuals responsible for health care reimbursement are best served by first mastering the fundamentals of health care insurance and then learning how to find resources to answer questions as they arise. There are three major types of health care insurance:

- Government insurance;
- Commercial for-profit insurance; and
- Non-governmental not-for-profit insurance.

These three types will be discussed separately in this chapter to give the reader a basic understanding of the structure and functionality of each.

GOVERNMENT INSURANCE

The federal government is the largest purchaser of health insurance in the United States. It offers three types of health care insurance to distinctive populations: Medicare, Medicaid, and TRICARE. Medicare insurance serves the elderly and disabled; Medicaid insures the indigent; and TRICARE (formerly known as the Civilian Health and Medical Program of the Uniformed Services [CHAMPUS]) is designed to cover U.S. military personnel and their dependents.

Medicare, Medicaid, and TRICARE are not-for-profit insurances. Medicare is a federal program that was established by Congress and is regulated at the federal level. Medicaid is state specific. While the federal government provides partial funding for Medicaid, each state legislates and regulates its own Medicaid program. TRICARE is provided federally and is the most straightforward of the government programs.

(*Note:* In addition to these three types of government insurance, the Federal Employees Health Benefit Plan [FEHBP] provides health insurance to federal employees. FEHBP depends on the concept of managed competition to provide insurance. *Managed competition* is a purchasing strategy rooted in the principles of competition to achieve the highest value possible to purchasers. FEHBP, because of its reliance upon managed competition and its similarity to commercial insurance plans, will not be specifically discussed.)

Medicare

Medicare insurance was instituted in 1965, but the impetus for the Medicare program dates back to the original Social Security Act passed in 1935. Although Medicare is tied to the Social Security program, it has its own multiple funding streams: mandatory contributions by employers and employees, general tax revenues, beneficiaries' premiums, and co-payments and deductibles. Title 18 of the Social Security Act designated Medicare as a complement to traditional Social Security benefits. Beneficiaries entitled to Medicare insurance under the Social Security Act include individuals who are 65 years of age or older, younger individuals with disabilities, and individuals with end stage renal disease (ESRD).

Medicare is divided into four parts: A, B, C, and D. Each of these parts governs different aspects of coverage. Because of the complexity of Medicare options, it is no wonder Medicare beneficiaries seek information from medical office insurance staff members who are associated with organizations they trust. While it is inappropriate for medical office insurance staff members to give advice regarding which plan to purchase, it is necessary for staff members to be knowledgeable about Medicare so that they can accurately answer questions. The following section outlines the different aspects of coverage in each Medicare part.

Medicare Parts A, B, C, and D

Medicare Part A is a fee-for-service plan that pays for hospital services including inpatient hospital services, skilled nursing facility services, home health care, and hospice care. The most comprehensive list of covered services under Part A is for inpatient hospital services. These services include a semi-private room, meals, special diets, nursing services, lab tests, X-ray and other radiology and radiation services, operating and recovery room services, special care units, medical supplies and equipment, in-patient drugs and blood transfusions, and rehabilitation services. Patients have a 90-day hospital care stay in a benefit period and have a 60-day lifetime reserve if the 90-day stay has been exhausted.

Medicare Part B insurance pays for physician services. Part B, called Supplemental Medical Insurance, is a fee-for-service plan that helps pay for outpatient hospital and ambulatory surgery center services, some home health services, and medical equipment and supplies. Part B also covers non-physician practitioner services, diagnostic tests, ambulance transportation, and certain preventive care services. Additional services covered include diagnostic tests, procedures related to treatment, radiology and pathology services, office visits with physicians' nurses, drugs and biologicals that cannot be self-administered such as chemotherapy, physical and occupational therapies, and speech pathology services.

Medicare Part C is known as Medicare Advantage. Part C, established by the Balanced Budget Act of 1997, is considered to be the Medicare managed care plan. Advantage plans are similar to health maintenance organizations (HMOs) or preferred provider organizations (PPOs). Part C offers broader coverage than the Part B fee-for-service plan. If an individual is eligible for both Medicare Part A and Part B, they may elect to have Part C coverage instead.

Medicare Part D is a voluntary drug benefit program that began in January 2006. Private insurance companies that are approved by Medicare provide Part D coverage. In order for a medication to be covered under Medicare, the service must be both reasonable and necessary for the diagnosis or treatment of the medical condition. Certain services are not covered, including those that have been excluded from the program as designated by the Centers for Medicare & Medicaid Services (CMS) and those that have not been approved by the Food and Drug Administration or are investigational in nature. Coverage benefits such as deductibles, premiums, and co-payments will depend on the plan that is chosen.

Actors in Medicare Claims Processing

The hierarchy of Medicare claims processing involves several actors. To negotiate this process effectively, it is essential to identify these actors and understand their respective roles:

- **The federal government.** The legislative branch of the federal government mandates Medicare program rules and regulations and appropriates money to run the Medicare program.

- **Medicare's administrative agencies.** In 2001, the administrative agency's name was changed from Health Care Financing Administration (HCFA) to Centers for Medicare & Medicaid Services (CMS). This organization is a part of the Department of Health and Human Services.

- **Non-governmental Medicare agencies.** Agencies contract with CMS to administer the Medicare program for all providers at a local, state, or regional level. An example of a contractor is the Wisconsin Physicians Services Insurance Corporation (WPS), which began as a Medicare Part B claims processor in 1966 in Wisconsin. Over the years WPS has expanded into several states including Illinois, Iowa, Kansas, Michigan, Minnesota, Missouri, and Nebraska to become one of the largest Medicare contractors. An additional expansion of services led WPS to join with Mutual of Omaha to have the capability of also processing Medicare Part A claims. Non-governmental organizations such as WPS contract to serve as the fiscal agent between providers and the federal government. They apply coverage rules to determine appropriate payment of claims.

  While WPS serves as a fiscal agent for Medicare Parts A and B, some contractors may only serve as contractors for institutions such as hospitals making payment determinations for Medicare Part A. Other contracts may make payment determinations for Medicare Part B professional services or may be a contractor acting as a fiscal agent for a durable medical equipment regional carrier. In the past, agencies administering Medicare Part A (that is, those that pay institutional organizations such as hospitals) have been called *fiscal intermediaries*. In contrast, agencies administering Medicate Part B (that is, those that pay for professional physician services) have been called *carriers*. Since 2005, new contracting agencies doing administration for all parts of Medicare are called *Medicare Administrative Contractors (MACs)*. By 2011 all contractors will have transitioned from their prior designation to the current MAC designation.

- **Hospitals.** Hospitals provide services under Medicare Part A and file claims with the MAC serving Medicare Part A for the region in which the hospital is located.

- **Physicians.** Physicians provide services under Medicare Part B and file claims with the MAC that is contracted to pay for those services based on the location the services are provided.

- **Medical insurance staff.** The medical insurance staff members who process claims in providers' organizations are important but often overlooked actors in the claims reimbursement process. Because they play an integral role on the front line of Medicare policy implementation and in determining costs to the Medicare program, it is necessary for these staff to be well trained and educated relating to Medicare.

Coverage Eligibility

Coverage eligibility for each part of Medicare is defined by the following criteria:

- **Medicare Part A.** An individual must be 65 years of age or older and be receiving or be eligible to receive retirement benefits from Social Security or the Railroad Retirement Board (RRB). Any person under age 65 must be eligible to receive disability benefits from Social Security or RRB for at least 24 months or be receiving dialysis or renal transplantation for ESRD.

- **Medicare Part B.** An individual must satisfy the criteria to be eligible for Medicare Part A and select enrollment in Medicare Part B. In most cases, Part B requires an individual to pay a monthly premium.

- **Medicare Part C.** An individual must be eligible for both Medicare Part A and Part B, as well as sign up during the normal enrollment period, which is usually within a seven-month window of time around his or her 65th birthday. Individuals may be turned down for Part C if they delay enrollment beyond the window of opportunity or do not qualify for health reasons. Medicare Part C Advantage Plans offer private health care options and are sometimes referred to as *managed care plans*.

- **Medicare Part D.** To qualify for Medicare Part D, an individual must be eligible for Medicare coverage. Enrollment in Medicare Part D usually requires an individual to pay a monthly premium; however, beneficiaries whose income is low enough to qualify for a subsidy are not required to pay a monthly premium. Medicare beneficiaries should enroll in Medicare Part D when they are first eligible for Part A Medicare, or they will be penalized when they decide to join.

Medicare Participation

Any provider who sees Medicare beneficiaries as patients is required to bill Medicare's limiting charge unless the provider is a Medicare participating provider. Participating physicians accept assignment on all Medicare claims and can expect payment from Medicare in 14 days. Medicare pays participating physicians 80 percent of the Medicare Allowable; the remaining 20 percent is collected from the patient.

The fee schedule for a non-participating provider is 95 percent of the fee schedule for a participating provider. In addition to receiving lower reimbursement, non-participating providers also must collect payment directly from the Medicare beneficiary instead of from Medicare. Claims filed by non-participating providers are referred to as *non-assigned claims*, and payment does not go directly to the provider. Therefore, it is beneficial for any physician intending to see Medicare patients to sign a participation agreement.

Once a physician has signed a participating physician or supplier agreement, the agreement renews automatically each year unless the provider notifies Medicare in writing that he or she wishes to terminate the agreement or the provider violates the agreement and is terminated by Medicare. Non-compliance with Medicare rules and regulations may incur civil and criminal penalties. Most medical practices providing services to large numbers of Medicare patients will want to become a participating provider to take advantage of the benefits of participation.

Site-of-Service Payment Consideration

Medicare reimbursement for some services varies depending on where the service is delivered to the patient. This determination is known as "site-of-service" payment consideration. Services that are usually performed in an office setting will be paid at a reduced amount, called a site-of-service reduction, if those services are performed elsewhere, such as in a hospital setting. This determination is based on the concept that services should be performed at the most appropriate facility to deliver the required care for a particular service.

Fee-for-Service Plans

Fee-for-service plans, which include Medicare Part A and Part B, allow beneficiaries to go to their choice of physician or hospital. The beneficiary is financially responsible to the provider for coinsurance payments, deductibles, any non-covered service, or services included in a written advanced notice. Fee-for-service beneficiaries may also have Medicaid and Medigap insurance to help pay for services. In order to qualify for Medicaid coverage, certain financial requirements must be met, and not all beneficiaries will qualify for Medicaid. On the other hand, Medigap is a supplemental insurance policy designed for any beneficiary who wishes to purchase a policy to help cover the expense of coinsurance that the beneficiary would otherwise be responsible for as an out-of-pocket expense.

Managed Care Plans

Managed care plans, which include Medicare Part C, typically require beneficiaries to receive health care from providers and hospitals identified by the managed care plan. Beneficiaries who qualify for Medicare Part A and Part B may participate in a Medicare Advantage plan (Part C), which are administered by private insurance carriers. If a beneficiary chooses to participate in an Advantage plan, the beneficiary must enroll in a plan that provides service where the beneficiary lives. In other words, a beneficiary cannot choose to be covered by a plan if the community in which he or she lives is not in the service area of that particular Advantage plan.

Payment Requests

Medicare Part A requires that beneficiaries pay a deductible at the beginning of each benefit period and pay coinsurance for most services. Coinsurance is based on the location of service and on the number of benefit days used. Medicare Part B requires beneficiaries to pay a yearly deductible that is subtracted from the approved amount of the first claim filed each year until the deductible amount is satisfied. Additionally, beneficiaries pay a 20 percent coinsurance for the allowed amount of covered services.

Advanced Beneficiary Notice

If a provider believes that Medicare may deny payment because Medicare standards may consider the service medically unnecessary, the provider must provide written notification to the Medicare beneficiary in advance of the service. If the provider intends the patient to be responsible for the bill, an Advanced Beneficiary Notice (ABN) must be signed indicating that the patient is aware of his or her financial responsibility. When filing the insurance claim on a service that the physician believes will be denied, the Current Procedural Terminology (CPT®)* GA modifier should be added to the billed service. A GA modifier on the claim form is used to signal to CMS that the provider has provided the Medicare beneficiary with an ABN to notify that the service will not likely be covered. An ABN form may be downloaded at www.cms.hhs.gov.

Non-Participating Providers

If a provider is not accepting assignment on a claim and the services provided will likely cost over $500, the provider must provide the Medicare beneficiary with an estimate of the charges in written form prior to providing the service. The written information advises the beneficiary of the estimated charges that are likely to be his or her responsibility. If a written estimate is not provided to the beneficiary, any money collected from the beneficiary must be refunded. If the refund is not made, civil monetary penalties and exclusion from the Medicare program may apply. Providers may opt to accept assignment on a per-claim basis. If assignment is not accepted, providers must collect payment for services from the beneficiary on non-assigned claims.

Primary and Secondary Payers

Medicare usually pays as the *primary* insurance in the absence of other insurance. Medicare may be the *secondary* payer if a patient has other insurances. These may include group health plan insurance, no-fault or liability insurance, workers' compensation, the Consolidated Omnibus Budget Reconciliation Act (COBRA) continuation coverage, Federal Black Lung Program, or military insurance from the U.S. Department of Veterans Affairs or TRICARE. There are several situations that result in Medicare as the secondary payer. One common situation arises when a beneficiary or spouse is working and covered under an employer group health plan; in this case, Medicare is the secondary insurance. In addition, when an individual is entitled to Medicare because of ESRD, Medicare is often the secondary insurance.

National Correct Coding Initiative

CMS developed the National Correct Coding Initiative (NCCI) to promote correct coding methodologies nationally and to control inappropriate payment on Medicare Part B claims due to improper coding. (*Note*: The acronyms NCCI and CCI are used interchangeably. NCCI information can be accessed online at www.cms.hhs.gov/NationalCorrectCodInitEd.) Correct Coding Initiative (CCI edits) give instruction about how and when codes should be reported, specifically what combinations are allowed, and which combinations are not allowed. CCI edits are used to prevent improper payment from incompatible combinations of codes. CCI edits allow certain modifiers that are found and defined in the current edition of the American Medical Association's *CPT* codebook. A more in-depth discussion of CCI edits is found in Chapter 3.

Enrollment in the Medicare Program — Providers

Providers wishing to enroll with Medicare must submit application forms appropriate for the services they will be providing to Medicare beneficiaries. In addition, a National Provider Identifier (NPI) application must be obtained before enrolling with Medicare. The Health Insurance Portability and Accountability Act (HIPAA) requires that each provider has an NPI number to be used on all standard claims transactions. This unique identifier replaces all other identifying numbers for providers and is broadly recognized by health plans. (*Note:* Signatures on the NPI application forms must be original — stamped signatures are not acceptable.) Enrollment tips can be found online at www. cms.hhs.gov/MedicareProvider/SupEnroll.

Enrollment in the Medicare Program — Beneficiaries

Beneficiary enrollment in Medicare may occur within a seven-month window around a beneficiary's 65th birthday — sign-up may occur any time during the beneficiary's 65th birthday month and the three months prior or three months after the birthday month. Beneficiaries may learn about signing up for Medicare services by going to the Social Security Administration Website or using the eligibility tool at www.medicare.gov.

Beneficiaries who sign up for Medicare receive Part A insurance to provide hospital coverage. Employment taxes paid while working entitles beneficiaries to

Medicare Part A without paying a monthly premium. Medicare Part B, which provides for physician services, is optional and must be selected. Unlike Part A, Part B requires a monthly premium. Part B also has an annual deductible. If beneficiaries are still covered by group health plan benefits when enrolling for Medicare Part A and decide to postpone taking Part B benefits, they may be required to pay a premium of up to 10 percent more for every year that they postponed electing Part B coverage.

Once participants sign up for Part B coverage, they are entitled to a one-time open enrollment period of six months, meaning that beginning at the time of enrollment for Part B they may choose any Medigap supplemental insurance plan regardless of their health for a six-month period. During that time frame, beneficiaries cannot be denied coverage under the Medigap plan selected. After the six-month open enrollment period, beneficiaries are subject to being excluded from the chosen Medigap policy due to medical conditions. Also, within the first six months of electing Part B coverage, each beneficiary is provided an initial preventive physical exam as well as screening for diabetes and heart disease.

Beneficiaries may select coverage options other than the original Medicare plan. Medicare beneficiaries may choose to be covered by some form of a Medicare Advantage plan. Medicare Advantage plans may include a variety of different coverage options such as Medicare HMOs, Medicare PPOs, Medicare Private-Fee-For-Service plans, or Medicare Medical Savings Account plans. Such a broad variety of options sometimes leaves beneficiaries confused about what will best suit their needs.

Medicare Website

Additional information regarding Medicare can be found online at www. cms.hhs.gov. This Website is massive, and the information you seek may not be easy to find. A tip for using the Website more effectively is to start at the Home screen and click Resources & Tools. Under Sitewide Tools and Resources, click Frequently Asked Questions and then enter the search term for which you need information. Information in this format is often easier to understand.

Medicaid

The Medicaid program is designed to provide medical benefits to certain low-income groups who have no or limited health care insurance. Medicaid does not cover all poor persons, as limited income is only one of the requirements for Medicaid coverage. The federal government establishes general guidelines for the Medicaid program, but each state is free to establish its own eligibility and benefits structure. The Medicaid program is administered by each state, and services vary by state.

Medicaid pays for medical services by sending reimbursement directly to the health care provider rather than sending money to the insured to pay for services. In some states, the Medicaid recipients are asked to pay a small portion of the fee for accessing services. The co-payment amounts, typically fifty cents to $3, vary by state as do the rules that determine income eligibility. As previously stated, income is only one of the determining criteria for Medicaid eligibility. The Federal Poverty Level Charts are used by state Medicaid agencies to help develop eligibility criteria.

Medicaid Eligibility Groups

Both federal and state law define Medicaid eligibility groups. Typically the eligibility groups are those that are characterized as categorically needy, medically needy, or special groups. It is important to note that not all states recognize all categories.

Categorically Needy. The categorically needy may not meet financial coverage thresholds but may be eligible for Medicaid because of excessive medical expenses. The categorically needy may be defined as:

- Families who meet the state eligibility requirements for Aid to Families with Dependent Children (AFDC);
- Low-income pregnant women and children under age six;
- Children ages 6–19 with a family income below the federal poverty level;
- Legal caretakers of low-income children;
- Supplemental Security Income (SSI) recipients; and
- Individuals living in medical institutions.

Medically Needy. Although not all states have medically needy programs, more than half of the states do provide such a program. The medically needy include:

- Those with too much money, income, or savings to be classified as categorically needy;
- Pregnant women through a 60-day postpartum period;
- Certain newborns and children under age 18;
- Persons who are aged, blind, or disabled (SSI may serve as a determining factor);
- Some groups of children under age 21 who meet requirements and are full-time students; and
- Individuals who would be eligible if they were not enrolled in a health maintenance organization.

Special Groups. Special groups may be defined as:

- Women who have breast or cervical cancer;
- People with tuberculosis (TB);
- Medicare beneficiaries; and
- Individuals who may have lost their Medicare coverage and are employed but are still below the federal poverty level.

Eligibility Time Frame

Medicaid coverage does not necessarily start the day an individual is approved for Medicaid. Coverage may start retroactively for up to three months prior to an individual's application, depending on the eligibility condition during the retroactive period. Medicaid coverage typically stops at the end of the month in which a person's circumstances change such that eligibility is affected.

Mandatory Services

While states dictate the services they provide and the limitations of those services, certain services are mandated by federal statute. Services provided must be available to everyone in that group unless they are explicitly waived under Medicaid law. Services for the categorically needy include:

- Inpatient hospital treatment;
- Outpatient hospital treatment;
- X-ray and labs;
- Services provided by state-licensed pediatric and family nurse practitioners;
- Nursing facility care if the beneficiary is age 21 or older;
- All medically necessary screening, diagnosis, and treatment if the beneficiary is under age 21;
- Family planning services;
- Physician services;
- Medical and surgical dentistry services;
- Home health care if the beneficiary is entitled to nursing facility care;
- Nurse–midwife services;
- Care during pregnancy and complicating conditions; and
- Postpartum care for 60 days.

Each state Medicaid program has unique requirements, and medical office insurance staff members should familiarize themselves with their own state's criteria. Each state has a Website outlining its services.

TRICARE

TRICARE is a worldwide health service with military facilities that provides health care services for military families through a network of civilian medical professionals. It provides benefits to military personnel and family members within five specific categories:

- Active duty service members and their family (even if the active duty service member is deceased);
- Retired service members and their families (even if the retired service member is deceased);
- Activated National Guard or Reserve members and their families;

- Non-activated National Guard or Reserve members and their families; and
- Retired National Guard or Reserve members and their families.

To receive TRICARE benefits an individual must be registered in the Defense Enrollment Eligibility Reporting System.

TRICARE recognizes both network and non-network providers. By law, non-network providers cannot charge more than 15 percent above the maximum allowable TRICARE fee schedule, and beneficiaries are not responsible to pay more than 15 percent. TRICARE may require prior authorization and some out-of-pocket costs to beneficiaries, but it will typically pay for any medical services that are considered proven and medically necessary.

TRICARE currently offers several health plan options. These options evolve as public law is amended. The most recent information regarding TRICARE can be found online at www.tricare.mil. Questions can be directed to regional contractors.

COMMERCIAL FOR-PROFIT INSURANCE

Health care costs can be unpredictable and expensive. For healthy individuals who require only preventive care, the cost of health care services may be minimal and the entire annual expenses for health care services inconsequential. However, an unexpected illness or accident can radically change the financial impact of health care expenses. Without insurance, someone suffering a serious injury or a chronic health condition requiring intensive or prolonged services may face the prospect of personal bankruptcy. Health care insurance is intended to help share expenses related to medical treatments and to give individuals the peace of mind in knowing that they can predict the range of financial outlay they will have related to medical services each year.

The assurance of financial protection drives most individuals to purchase health care insurance if financially feasible. The unique aspect of health insurance in the United States is that health insurance is primarily tied to employment through group health plans. Benefits are selected at a management level on an annual basis, and the selected benefits are offered to employees of the organization at a monthly premium established by the employer.

The type of health care insurance offered (see Exhibit 1.1) and the regulations pertaining to health care insurance have evolved over the years. Massive changes have occurred in health care insurance primarily because of the implementation of Medicare in 1965. Medicare, intended as a safety net against high health care cost for seniors, has proven to be the driving force behind most health care insurance changes affecting all age communities in the United States.

As insurance coverage has evolved, so too have the expectations of the American people. It is generally agreed that the current health care system is inadequate to meet these expectations. A little history should help us understand how we got here.

EXHIBIT 1.1 ■ Major Categories of Commercial Insurance

Category	Definition
Fee-for-Service (FFS)	Typically indemnity insurance, insurance pays 80%, insured pays 20%.
Discounted Fee-for-Service	Provider gives carrier discount on standard fee, discount is passed on to insured.
Managed Care HMOs	Designed to provide cost savings by exerting effort to control access to services by requiring referrals and pre-certification. May require primary care gatekeeper.
Managed Care PPOs	Designed to provide cost savings, emphasize in-network care. Usually no gatekeeper. Features of both FFS and HMO.
Managed Care POSs	Designed to provide cost savings, emphasize in-network care. Require gatekeeper. Features of both FFS and HMO.

Fee-for-Service Plans

Health care insurance of the 1960s was largely indemnity insurance that paid 80 percent of the fee-for-service charge submitted by the health care provider while the insured paid the remaining 20 percent of the billed charge. During that time deductibles were low ($200 or less) and patients were free to choose their own provider. Usually, with indemnity fee-for-service, insurance patients could not only choose their primary care provider but also they had the flexibility to choose to see a specialist without a referral and could opt to change health care providers at any time.

The closest relative to the traditional fee-for-service plan is the discounted fee-for-service plan. In this arrangement a health insurance carrier initiates a contracted rate with health care providers to provide services at a discounted percentage of their standard fee. For example, a carrier may contract with a provider to pay at 85 percent of billed charges. That gives the carrier a discount of 15 percent that is passed on to the purchaser of the carrier's insurance plan. This may seem to be a good arrangement for all parties because the arrangement is simple and straightforward without engaging in complex contract negotiations. However, this arrangement does not ensure predictable cost saving in purchasing health care services because providers are at liberty to adjust their fee schedules to keep up with the rising cost of practicing medicine. This is particularly true with costs related to supplies and labor. In reality, traditional insurance plans lacked the ability to control costs, creating an opportunity for innovations in health care insurance such as networks of providers in which insurers could exert more control over cost.

In the 1970s the cost of medical care was increasing. The United States was beginning to see high utilization of health care services and was simultaneously on the brink of the explosion of technological advances in medicine. In 1973 legislation was passed to provide federal funding for the expansion of HMOs to address rising health care costs that were influenced in part by high utilization and the availability of advanced technology. What seemed then like unparalleled increases in cost made it important for insurance carriers, both government and commercial, to engage in cost containment and cost savings measures. Since the 1980s the growth of managed care has continued to increase dramatically. By the 1990s most Americans' health care insurance was in some form of managed care plan, and by the beginning of the 21st century only a small percentage of Americans in employee-sponsored health plans were covered by traditional indemnity fee-for-service insurance plans.

Managed Care Plans

Because of the emphasis on cost containment, employers and individuals have welcomed the growth of managed care, and many managed care arrangements are available to the American public. Managed care plans are offered at lower costs than the indemnity fee-for-service plans and provide an opportunity to tailor health care benefits that better fit the needs of the insured.

For the insured there are several important considerations of any health care insurance plan — the monthly premium, co-payment amounts, deductible amount, the amount insurance pays for covered services, and coinsurance (see Exhibit 1.2). Unfortunately many insured do not understand the role of each element. Too many believe that because they pay a large monthly premium, for example, their health care services are already covered without any further financial burden to them. In fact, in employer-sponsored group health plans, the monthly employee contribution is determined by the employer and assessed to the insured employee. Paying the monthly contribution, deducted from payroll, does not ensure anything other than providing the employee with health care insurance. Health care insurance is good assurance of access to medical care provided at a discounted rate — all else is based on the benefit package.

The next element of insurance is the co-payment. The co-pay is a charge amount that will be paid by the insured upon accessing services as designated by benefit design. Initially when co-pays were introduced they were small amounts in the range of $5–10 and were attached to physician visits but rarely to screening or diagnostic services. Arrangements relating to co-pays have been altered significantly. Co-pays have increased several fold, and they may be attached to both visits and tests. Some employers have opted out of co-pays because the amount of money spent in co-pays does not contribute to meeting one's deductible.

EXHIBIT 1.2 ■ Fundamental Elements of Health Insurance

Fundamental	How it Works
Premium	Paid monthly during contract year. Price based on contracted benefits to pay portion of insured's health services as outlined in benefits package. Paid by insured before insurance pays.
Co-payment	Required payment when services are accessed. Stipulated by benefits package. Paid by insured before insurance pays.
Deductible	Self-insured portion of health insurance. Must be met before health insurance begins to pay. Re-set with each plan year. Paid by insured before insurance pays.
Insurance Payment	The portion of health care services paid by insurance carrier. The amount paid is based on the benefits package purchased. Payment varies based on whether services were in-network or out-of-network.
Coinsurance	The service balance that remains after health care insurance has paid. The insured is responsible for this amount.

Deductibles are the self-insured portion of insurance and, like co-pays, have increased considerably over time. High-deductible health plans have shifted cost away from the insurance carrier and onto the insured. In some cases the employer has assumed some responsibility for a portion of the deductible by establishing HRAs for employees. In any case, high deductible plans have lowered the cost of yearly and monthly premiums for the employer and the employee. Only after the deductible has been met will insurance pay. The amount of the billed charge that insurance pays is based on the negotiated rate of the contract with the provider. That negotiated rate, known as the *allowable amount*, is the medium that assures the insured a guaranteed discount on health care services. The insurance carrier starts with the negotiated allowable amount and pays a percentage of the allowable amount to the provider. The percentage paid is dictated by the benefits package purchased by the employer.

Last, to resolve the cost of the medical service, the employee is responsible for coinsurance. The coinsurance percentage varies based on whether the health care provider of services is in-network or out-of-network. Network services have been negotiated between the insurance carrier and health care providers. Services provided in-network are subject to the contracted allowable amount and represent predictable costs to the insurance carrier. Network services are less costly to the insured than out-of network services. Out-of-network services will cost the insured more based on the terms of the benefit structure outlined by the insurance carrier. Further, because the provider is not a participating provider, under contract with the insurance carrier, the provider may not be willing to accept the allowed amount paid by the insurance carrier. As a result, the patient is responsible for the cost difference between the allowed amount and the standard fee of the provider. It is understandable that insured patients are sometimes as complicated and difficult for a medical practice's insurance staff members to deal with as uninsured patients.

The common types of managed care are HMOs, PPOs, and point-of-service (POS) plans. Managed care plans provide a wide range of services and focus on reducing costs by requiring the insured to seek health care from network providers who have contracted with the health plan. Two other attempts at cost control are utilization review, which is designed to control the number of times a patient sees a provider, and requiring a referral from a primary care provider before the patient can see a specialist.

Health Maintenance Organizations

Traditionally HMOs are considered to focus on preventive care and can work well for healthy populations — sometimes HMOs are referred to as "well-care insurance." HMOs can provide significant cost savings in health plan benefits for employers. HMOs usually require the insured to receive services from a network provider with which the HMO has a contract. HMOs typically exert considerable effort to control access to services by requiring referrals for certain services and pre-certification for hospital admission.

Preferred Provider Organizations

PPOs are similar to HMOs in that they are designed to provide cost savings, but they incorporate some of the features of fee-for-service insurance, and they usually cost more than HMOs. In most cases PPOs do not require a primary care provider to act as a patient's gatekeeper but do provide lists of certain providers from which the insured can choose. PPOs emphasize seeking care from a network provider and sometimes require written referrals before seeing a specialist. The coinsurance charge for the insured will be higher if the insured receives care from a provider that is out-of-network.

Point-of-Service Plans

POS plans, like PPOs, incorporate features of both fee-for-service and HMO plans. In fact, POS plans are like PPOs except that POS plans require a gatekeeper primary care provider who coordinates care for the insured. Because PPO and POS plans incorporate features of fee-for-service insurance, both types of managed care are more expensive than HMO plans.

Although managed care plans tend to insure populations less likely to use health care services at the same rate of utilization as older age populations, managed care options have still not succeeded in reducing costs to acceptable rates. Dissatisfaction has given rise to consumer-directed health plans such as

EXHIBIT 1.3 ■ Self-Insured Plans Benefits Comparison

Internal Revenue Service (IRS) Plan Design	Flexible Savings Account—FSA	Health Reimbursement Account—HRA	Health Savings Account—HSA
Who Qualifies?	Qualify if employer provides	Qualify if employer provides	Anyone with HDHP—including self-employed
Requires High Deduct-ibe Health Plan (HDHP)	No	No	Yes
Contribution Limits	None	None	Set yearly by IRS
When is Money Used?	Anytime	Employer decides	Anytime
Salary Tax Status	Pre-tax allowed	Pre-Tax not allowed except with HDHP offered with HRA	Allowed for pre-tax with HDHP and after tax
Carryover	No carryover for unused amounts—Use in calendar year	Permitted	Required
Medical Expenses Covered	Unreimbursed medical expenses defined by IRS Code 213(d). No insurance premiums or Long-term care (LTC) services.	Unreimbursed medical expenses defined by IRS Code 214(d). Insurance premiums and LTC.	Unreimbursed medical expenses defined by IRS Code 213(d). COBRA premiums, qualified LTC, and insurance premiums while receiving unemployment benefits over age 65.
Preventive Care	Allowed	Allowed	Allowed by HDHP statute
Health Insurance Status	Not required to have insurance to participate	Employer decides	Yes, must have HDHP
Who Contributes?	Employee, employer, or both	Employee decides, Employer mandatory	Employee or employer
Cash Out of Unused Amount	No	No	Permitted but with tax consequences unless 65+
Portability—job to job	No	Employer decides	Yes
Medical Expenses Year of Contribution	Yes	No	No
Annual Amount Available 1st Day of Coverage	Yes	No	No
Other Insurance Limited	No	No	Yes
Taxable Account Earnings	No	No	No, but cash-out may be taxed
Who Sets Up?	Employer	Employer	Employer

health reimbursement accounts (HRAs), health savings accounts (HSAs), and flexible spending accounts (FSAs) that are designed to offset unreimbursed medical expenses (see Exhibit 1.3).

Health Reimbursement Accounts. HRAs are insurance plans partially self-funded by the insured's employer, who pays a premium up to a cap. The employer receives business expense tax savings when distributions are made. After the cap has been reached, the traditional insurance policy kicks in. HRAs, also known as *health reimbursement arrangements*, do not have any health insurance requirements and look like traditional insurance to the insured. HRAs are largely designed at the discretion of the employer, and only employers can make contributions. While employers may seek employee input into HRA design, the employer has the discretion to make benefit design decisions. The insured typically pays physician co-pays, drug card co-pays, deductibles, and coinsurance.

Health Savings Accounts. The Medicare Prescription Drug, Improvement, and Modernization Act of 2003 provided for HSAs. HSAs are a medical savings account that participants fund with before-tax dollars. The money in an HSA can be used for both current and future qualified medical expenses. Savings not spent within the year in which the contribution is made can be carried over for use in future years. HSAs are coupled with high deductible health plans in which deductibles and out-of-pocket expenses are defined and adjusted annually and do not allow participants to be covered by secondary insurance. HSAs allow both individuals and employers to make contributions to the account, and the HSA is portable. HSAs place spending responsibility on the individual. They differ from HRAs, in which no separate savings account is established.

Flexible Spending Accounts. FSAs, also known as *flexible spending arrangements*, are set up by employers to allow employees to use pre-tax dollars, set aside through payroll deduction, to pay for unreimbursed qualified medical expenses. While usually funded by employees, employers may also contribute. Like HRAs, there is no insurance requirement for participation. Money in an FSA must be withdrawn for services provided within the calendar year in which the money is set aside. Any unused funds are forfeited to the employer. Unlike HSAs, FSAs are not portable.

COBRA

Any employees covered by employer-sponsored health insurance who leave their employment, whether voluntarily or involuntarily, are able under federal law to maintain the insurance coverage provided by their employer. The Consolidated Omnibus Budget Reconciliation Act of 1985 (COBRA) dictates that employers with 20 or more employees must offer continued health insurance coverage to former qualified employees or their families who wish to maintain insurance coverage. COBRA allows employers to charge the insured up to 102 percent of the monthly premium to maintain coverage. COBRA coverage in most cases can be extended for 18 months if the employer is informed of the intent to be covered by COBRA within 60 days from the date employment was terminated and the premium is paid in full. Even employees who are not qualified to maintain health insurance under federal COBRA may be able to qualify under state law that covers an employee working for an employer with fewer employees than the federal COBRA requirement. State law will verify the state-specific requirements to qualify for small-group COBRA.

Workers' Compensation

Employees who are hurt or become ill in a work-related accident qualify for workers' compensation insurance benefits. Workers' compensation requires employers to pay premiums based on industry classification. The Workers' Compensation Board (WCB) — a neutral agency that resolves workers' compensation issues — administers workers' compensation insurance. Employees who believe that they have a workers' compensation claim must notify their employer immediately. Upon notification, the employer will have the employee complete paperwork relating to the event in order to file a claim.

Typically benefits covered by workers' compensation insurance require employers to be responsible for a portion — usually two thirds — of lost wages related to the injury or illness as well as all direct cost of medical treatment.

Workers' compensation regulations are state specific. That may mean that not all employers in a state are required to provide workers' compensation insurance for their employees. Federal law focuses on non-military federal employees and companies engaged in interstate commerce. Although state law is not bound to federal law, federal law sets the coverage standards for the states. The influence of federal law is evidenced in various other federal laws that pertain to broad groups of employees other than those covered by workers' compensation. These laws address requirement for companies engaged in specific types of commerce conducted broadly, particularly across state lines.

If employees collect workers' compensation benefits, generally they are giving up the right to sue their employer. Workers' compensation insurance is intended to protect employers from lawsuits if they have maintained a standardized, safe work environment. In addition to protecting employers, workers' compensation insurance also protects co-workers from liability. The key information for medical office insurance staff members relating to workers' compensation insurance is to know that the employer must verify that the workers' compensation carrier will cover medical expenses.

Direct Contracting

Health insurance coverage may also be obtained through direct contracting. Under direct contracting, the employer arranges for health services directly with a provider, outside of the framework of a commercial health care plan. In practice, direct contracting is widely discussed but is not widespread. It works best with very large employers who are interested in working with local organizations to deliver health care services. While direct contracting can be successful in certain situations, it causes employers and providers to perform roles that they may not have the infrastructure to support, such as risk management and other functions of an insurance company. Direct contracting may work best when a third-party administrator (TPA) is hired to handle the administrative issues. However, employers may be reluctant to engage with a TPA if they consider a large part of the high cost of managed care plans to be administrative costs. The percentage of each dollar that is designated for administrative cost has often been a source of frustration for employers.

From the provider perspective, direct contracting is considered to be similar to capitation, where a set premium is paid for treating some or all members of a group for a designated period of time. This kind of per-member per-month arrangement has not proven to work well in many markets, and providers may not meet this aspect of direct contracting enthusiastically. Nevertheless, while negotiating a direct contract is difficult because of the competing interests, direct contracting is a viable option for some markets.

NON-GOVERNMENTAL NOT-FOR-PROFIT INSURANCE

In contrast to governmental programs and commercial for-profit insurance, health insurance may come in the form of non-governmental not-for-profit programs. These programs vary in size and function and are typically created due to a community need. Started to shore needy citizens in the community, these insurance programs often serve as a safety net for the otherwise uninsured. They remove the barriers of access to health care for various groups of people and, in doing so, improve the overall health of the community. Some insurance organizations remain as community or county products, while others expand to statewide and beyond. Examples of some not-for profit community insurance programs are: Community Health Plan of Washington, Community Health Group in San Diego, Univera Community Health in New York, and Fallon Community Health Plan in Worcester, Massachusetts.

Original Blue Cross Blue Shield

The precursor of Blue Cross and Blue Shield (BCBS) began in Texas in 1929. Dr Justin Kimball, who was a former school superintendent, became an administrator at Baylor Hospital in Dallas. The economic times were hard, and when Dr Kimball looked at the accounts receivable of the hospital he recognized names that he was familiar with from the school system. His knowledge of the low wages in the school system inspired an idea that laid out the roadmap for employer-sponsored health care insurance in the United States.

Dr Kimball set up a plan that would guarantee teachers a hospital stay up to 21 days for a premium of 50 cents per month. The success of the plan caused it to be copied by hospitals throughout the nation and, by 1944, Dr Kimball's idea became known as Blue Cross and Blue Shield of Texas. The plan expanded from teachers to everyone with a job. The evolution of Blue Cross Blue Shield insurance from its humble beginning to the broad range of product offerings of today mirrors the changes that have occurred with health insurance nationwide. The innovative idea of Dr Kimball to start affordable health insurance coverage for average working Americans revolutionized health care coverage and is the legacy of today's health insurance industry.

BCBS began as a not-for-profit organization. The Blue Cross became so synonymous with hospital coverage that the American Hospital Association began to use it to denote high-quality hospital plans. Initially Blue Shield was used to signify medical plans, but today in most markets there is no separation in hospital and medical coverage. Not only is BCBS the oldest health plan in the United States, it is the largest and has the broadest coverage — all 50 states and beyond.

BCBS was instrumental in the start up of Medicare by providing the infrastructure to administer the Medicare program. Still today, BCBS's ties to the federal government are strong; BCBS continues to administer the Medicare program in many regions and is the largest carrier providing health care insurance coverage to employees insured by the FEHBP. Although BCBS started as a non-for-profit insurance, today it has evolved and is involved in every legitimate organizational structure, including publicly traded companies, offering every legitimate type of health care insurance.

Private Not-for-Profits

Like BCBS in its beginning, there are many socially minded organizations that have set up private non-for-profit health insurance companies to help safeguard citizens. These private not-for-profit organizations hope to provide protection from the risk of being driven into bankruptcy because of high medical bills, and they advocate on individuals' behalf when they are unable to be their own advocate. Many of these plans are area, state, or region specific and may have religious or community affiliations. The range of coverage offered by these plans is varied. Some plans may provide small sums to help pay premiums, co-pays, deductibles, coinsurance, and/or COBRA. Other plans may offer a full array of health plans — traditional insurance, PPO, POS, workers' compensation, and others. Private not-for-profits do not necessarily look alike or fill one intended role; their greatest similarity is their tax-exempt status.

References

1. American Medical Association, *CPT 2008* (Chicago: American Medical Association, 2008).

2. Ingenix, "Introduction," in *Medicare Correct Coding Guide*, January 2009. Page 3.

CHAPTER TWO

Understanding Medical Office Insurance Staff

This chapter provides insights gleaned from a qualitative study of medical office insurance staff working in both large and small practices.[1] The study focused on how medical office insurance staff members make decisions relating to reimbursement for physicians' offices and how, in turn, they implement policy relating to reimbursement. More generally, the study sought an understanding of how complexity influences organizations, or, in other words, how medical office insurance staff members make sense of ambiguous and complex situations.

MEDICAL OFFICE INSURANCE STAFF ACT AS STREET-LEVEL BUREAUCRATS

In their daily work, medical office insurance staff members exhibit behaviors and skills characteristic of what social scientists call "street-level bureaucrats." The central characteristic of street-level bureaucrats is their use of discretion. When compared to bureaucrats who work in a highly scripted manner, street-level bureaucrats understand that the use of discretion is not only legitimate but also necessary to the reality of their work. Street-level bureaucrats work in unstructured environments in which the rules are unclear. In this setting, adaptation to circumstances is reasonable, and decisions require the use of general problem-solving techniques because many situations are unique and unscripted. On the other hand, bureaucrats work in very structured environments in which decisions are programmed based on routine organizational processes.

While discretion is the main defining characteristic of street-level bureaucrats, a second characteristic is autonomy from organizational authority. Street-level bureaucrats develop this characteristic because of the kind of work that they do and the positions they hold within the organization. Social researcher, Michael Lipsky, who noted these defining characteristics of street-level bureaucrats, also pointed out that the working conditions of street-level bureaucrats often include:[2]

- Inadequate resources;
- Increases in demand for services when the supply of services increases;
- Ambiguous, vague, or conflicting goal expectations;
- Difficult-to-measure goal achievement performance; and
- Non-voluntary clients.

Medical office insurance staff members typically interact with benefit recipients directly at the point where the service is delivered. They are in a position to exercise significant discretion over the lives of the people whom they serve. The work of medical office insurance staff requires judgment because it is so complicated — it is impossible to write hard and fast rules that cover all of the situations staff members will deal with in the course of their work.

Generally, the resources of medical office insurance staff members are inadequate to deal with the volume of work they are required to process. This lack of resources means that staff may develop coping skills to handle the work they do, and they may operate independently without direct supervision from management. As a result, the relationship between managers and medical office insurance staff can be edgy. Managers who are tasked to resolve the inadequate resources issue may be unable to do so because of organizational constraints. As such, they must allow medical office insurance staff members to work according to their own judgment and preferences.

In addition, managers may also be willing to focus on work achievement and ignore the amount of autonomy that insurance staff exercises as long as production is high. When medical office insurance staff members produce good revenues, managers may be willing to overlook the insurance department. Even when revenues are not good, managers may often be at a loss as to how to investigate what is going wrong. Managers who understand the nature of the work of the medical office insurance staff will be in a better position to interact most effectively with staff members in the insurance department.

Charged by the organization to get money in the door by processing claims accurately and quickly, medical office insurance staff members take information from clients, review and submit that information, and relate the results of their efforts to clients who are directly affected by those efforts. This process is filled with ambiguity and complexity. Inherent in this dynamic is the fact that health care insurance, both private and government funded, is the primary source of income for services rendered by physicians in medical practices.

While physicians depend on health care insurance for reimbursement for services, the insured patient depends on health care insurance to cover the bulk of purchased health care services. Patients covered by health insurance from government-sponsored programs or from employer-sponsored health insurance as an employee benefit assume that they will be responsible for little, if any, of the cost of their health care services. Patient expectations reflect the notion that health care services are rendered for a fee because they are covered by insurance.

Based on the fee-for-services premise, the encounter is not complete once the patient receives services from the physician. Rather, it requires that members of the medical office insurance staff orchestrate the process and perform the administrative functions that are necessary to complete the patient/provider encounter. These staff members deal with all non-clinical aspects of the patient's visit to the health care provider, including coverage by government insurance payers and private insurance payers. The staff members must use inductive reasoning to try to make sense of the ambiguity inherent in the non-standardized process while at the same time processing large volumes of claims. Medical office staff members are faced with the multiple objectives of bringing maximum revenue into the organization while at the same time processing the claims accurately and quickly.

INFORMATION PROCESSING BY MEDICAL OFFICE INSURANCE STAFF

For the process of reimbursement from insurance carriers to work correctly, several conditions must be met at two distinct junctures in the medical facility, each of which presents situations of ambiguity for the medical office insurance staff. At the first juncture, the medical office insurance staff members must have access to the patient's insurance card and must interpret the information on the card correctly so that the information put into the office's computer system is accurate. Only if the information is processed correctly can the physician obtain payment from the insurance carrier. However, if the insurance information is not processed correctly, the insurance carrier will not issue correct payment to the physician and, in some cases, the patient may be held responsible for the services.

The insurance card can be a confusing source of information. Optimally, an insurance card should contain several pieces of information to assist in proper claim filing; however, because a standardized format for insurance cards has not been mandated in the United States, there is wide disparity between insurance cards. Some insurance cards bear all of the required information, while others lack information. Staff must learn to search for and identify the critical pieces of information. Because electronic verification of insurance coverage is not widely available, medical office staff members are forced to make sense of the insurance card process in order for the physician to get paid and the beneficiary to be able to collect benefits. (See Chapter 3 for more information about medical insurance cards.)

Adding to the potential for confusion, patients often have both primary and secondary insurance. Medical office insurance staff must make the determination of which insurance is primary and which is secondary. Patients often cannot identify and distinguish their primary and secondary insurance carriers. Medicare has rules distinguishing situations in which Medicare is primary from those in which it is secondary, which will be discussed further in Chapter 3.

In addition to gathering the correct information for filing claims from the insurance card, medical office insurance staff members face a second crossroads at the time when the insurance carrier remits payment for medical services. A form, known as an explanation of benefits (EOB) form, accompanies each remittance for an insurance claim. The staff members must interpret the EOB precisely in order to apply the payment accurately against the charge for services rendered. Like insurance cards, however, EOBs also do not have a standardized format, and insurance staff must review them carefully to obtain all of the information needed to apply the payment and to detect any potential errors on the part of the insurance company.

Similar to insurance cards, incongruity exists in EOB formats. EOBs may be difficult to read, they may not contain the specific information needed to apply the payment, and they may reflect incorrect benefit pricing. A medical facility must be able to tie the reimbursement from an EOB to the proper charges for credit application. This matching is done by a patient's name, date of birth, and/or social security number. The information on an EOB differs from the information on an insurance card in that the EOB must refer to the date of service, place of service, services provided for payment application, and attending physician. Like insurance cards, the format and information contained on EOB forms vary from carrier to carrier. Because the information can be convoluted, the medical staff members processing payment from an insurance carrier are faced with pervasive ambiguity. (Reading and interpreting EOBs is discussed further in Chapter 4.)

The medical office insurance staff members are forced at these two important junctures — obtaining information from patient insurance cards and EOB forms — to create a coherent process from an incoherent product. They work in an unpredictable environment filled with ambiguity and complexity. Tasks often do not follow a prearranged standard, creating a need for staff members to make sense of tasks at hand. They are required to be flexible and use discretion to meet the challenge of their positions in the organization. Also, it should be noted that the rules and regulations applying to government payers do not necessarily govern private carriers. Yet, medical office insurance staff members are forced to work in an environment where both private and government payers coexist.

KEY CHALLENGES FOR MEDICAL OFFICE INSURANCE STAFF

In the medical office, claims are filed with the expectation that they will be paid. But medical office insurance staff members find that "working denials" of claims is a large-scale, time-consuming part of their job. Thus, they are often put into the position of adjudicating conflicting interpretations of policy and procedure.

Medical office insurance staff members primarily work in situations of information overload and in which external forces constrain behavior. These conditions are conducive to unexpected events that present many key challenges and can cause feelings of frustration for the medical office insurance staff.

Adhering to External Regulation

"If you don't have the documentation to cover it, don't charge it…"

Although medical office insurance staff members act with discretion and autonomy, their actions are often bound by external forces or forces beyond their control. External forces may come in the form of either persons or regulations. Individuals both within and outside of the organization, as well as regulations both internal and external to the organization, can serve as forces over which medical office insurance staff members have no control.

Staff members make many references to the effect of external forces on their behavior. For example, staff members understand that if they don't have the documentation to support charging a service, the service can't be charged. Medical office staff members charged with making sure that revenue comes into the organization must exercise restraint by not overstepping their bounds when the physician's obligations for documentation are not thoroughly satisfied.

The possibility of non-compliance with Medicare is particularly worrisome to medical office insurance staff. Breaching Medicare regulations can have serious consequences such as penalties, fines, and practice restrictions. Medical office insurance staff members are particularly vulnerable to mistakes because they process a large volume of claims, many of which fall outside of the standard of processing a "clean" insurance claim.

Insurance staff members consider a claim's circumstantial factors, weigh the consequences of the alternatives, and use discretion to withhold a charge rather than risk creating charges for services that do not have supporting documentation. The majority of staff members consider compliance with Medicare regulations to be more significant in defining their limits than an organizational directive.

Although physicians and managers influence staff behavior, there is no indication that medical office insurance staff members influence physician behavior. For example, the ramifications of the mistakes made at the front desk are more work for the medical office insurance staff members whose resources are too scarce to compensate for those mistakes. Staff members report that too often management does not intervene with corrective action at the front desk. This situation sets up a relationship between staff and managers that is characterized by intrinsic conflict and mutual dependence. Because management represents an external force that medical office insurance staff members cannot control, staff members develop coping skills to accommodate inadequate office processes and compensate in such ways as creating a "cheat sheet" for the front desk office staff to use to help eliminate some of the mistakes at the front desk.

Medical office insurance staff members are affected by rules and regulations that, if violated, could cause severe problems such as fines and penalties for their organizations. Medical office insurance staff members, sensitive to these issues, focus on areas of greatest risk to the organization. They express concern about their boundaries and prefer to err on the side of compliance even if it costs their organization revenue. The correct code is billed in an attempt to follow Medicare's correct coding practices. Further, staff members recognize that they must follow Medicare regulations and be aware of issues that the Office of Inspector General (OIG) is investigating. The OIG is charged to safeguard the integrity of the Department of Health and Human Services programs so it falls to OIG to investigate fraud and abuse. Insurance staff members are concerned about filing erroneous claims and suggest that a patient who seems to be involved in a dishonest scheme be told about insurance fraud.

Staff members, bound by external forces, associate and disassociate themselves with behaviors in order to not threaten their own identity in the organization. These external forces create situations that cannot be handled through routine procedures and require medical office members to define their own limits in dealing with these situations.

Coping with Information Overload

"Cards may have as many as three payers…"

"You have 60 patients…"

Information overload is defined by social scientist Karl Weick as "a complex mixture of the quantity, ambiguity, and variety of information that people are forced to process."[3] Unquestionably, the act of processing medical insurance is fraught with too much information. Medical office insurance staff members are the key actors in processing medical insurance and are actively involved in both input and output of information. They, more than all of the other actors involved in the medical insurance process, must filter insurance information for correctness, compatibility, and compliance. Incorrect information will result in a claim that does not get paid or gets paid incorrectly, and that results in a problem for both the organization and the patient.

Staff members try to fix errors and refile claims. An insurance claim that contains incompatible information can also become a problem for the patient and the organization. Not only will the organization not get paid correctly, but also staff members will be held responsible by both the patient and the insurance carrier to correct the incompatibility. This correction can become a lengthy and arduous process. For example, a Medicare agent may say that the claim was not paid because it was filed incorrectly, perhaps because of a wrong diagnosis or wrong procedure, and insurance staff must then send the information back to the clinic for it to verify what was actually done so that the claim can be refiled. Clearly, this is a time-consuming process for insurance staff.

First, some information may be incorrect because patients presented wrong information at the front desk. In addition, the volume of information processed by the front desk increases the likelihood of mechanical errors such as normal keying errors. The volume, coupled with the non-standardization of insurance cards, creates a situation ripe for mistakes. Insurance cards may have as many as three payers listed on them, and the front desk personnel must decide which insurance is primary and which is secondary. If the wrong decision is made, the office won't get paid without refilling the claim. Further, employers change health care insurance often and sometimes employees don't have the appropriate information about their current health care insurance carrier. Also, insurance companies often merge with other carriers or change names. It is no wonder staff members often have a difficult time staying on top of these tasks.

Second, information generated from medical services can be problematic. The service code, procedure codes, and the diagnosis codes must be compatible. Some procedures can be charged with a visit code under certain circumstances, but most cannot. Sometimes patients have tests in the organization at the time of the visit. When patients have tests, the medical office insurance staff must know that information for proper billing and claim filing. Sometimes patients have multiple diagnoses, and staff members must include all diagnoses and know which one is the primary diagnosis. Medical office insurance staff members act as detectives, synthesizing information in order to minimize ambiguity.

Third, after the response to a claim has been made there is additional work to be done to determine whether or not the claim was paid correctly. The response to the claim must be made in terms of deductibles, coinsurance, payment, adjustments, denials, refiling, and secondary filing. This contributes to the impression of information overload. In an attempt to process this information, it is often necessary to contact the insurance carrier. Feedback from the carrier can alter the information they began with. Staff must note what information stayed the same and what changed. This activity helps make sense of information overload.

The rules governing Medicare policy are larger in volume than the IRS code. Yet, medical office insurance staff members, who are products of on-the-job training, are responsible to appropriately apply Medicare rules and regulations to a myriad of situations. Failure on the part of staff members puts the organization and its physicians at risk. Staff members realize that whatever they do incorrectly will affect the clinic, and they understand unequivocally that it is their responsibility to get the claim filed correctly. Most often, medical office insurance staff members do not have adequate personal resources, such as education or training, to deal with the issues they face, nor do they have the organizational resources, such as enough personnel, to efficiently and effectively deal with a system whose processes are so complicated and elusive. These individuals develop a coping skill known in social science as "muddling through." Medical office insurance staff members, understanding the complexity inherent in their work, know that their work is too complicated to know everything they must know. They will, by default, notice some aspects of their work and ignore other aspects as they muddle through the volumes of claims they process.

Managing Frustration

> *"I do a lot of fighting with insurance companies..."*

Often feelings of frustration are caused by the working situations of medical office insurance staff. It is to be expected that a working environment composed of ambiguous regulations coupled with work overload and limited resources would create such feelings. Medical office insurance staff members are forced to manage this frustration in order to remain in their jobs.

Often staff members focus blame on insurance companies as the root cause of much of their frustration. "It is so typical of the insurance companies to pay all of the claim but a charge or two"; "I do a lot of fighting with insurance companies"; "I'm taking on the insurance companies"; "I'm not afraid to confront them"; and "I am just about ready to kill somebody" may be common statements overheard in a medical office by the insurance staff. When they discuss the difficulty of getting information from insurance carriers, they refer to their work as "detective work" in which they "investigate" a situation that "requires some leg work" because insurance companies treat information as if it is a "huge secret."

Staff members may use metaphors to express frustration about the imprecise nature and complexity of their work. They may speak of "muddling issues," doing a "juggling act," and refer to themselves as, "Jack of all trades." These references reveal their perception of the ambiguity and complexity of their work that requires them to "dig in" and "figure out" how to handle each individual situation. The frustration that medical office insurance staff members experience in their work situations leads them to try to make sense of the activities they are involved in during the course of their work.

RESULTING CHARACTERISTICS OF MEDICAL OFFICE INSURANCE STAFF

The high levels of frustration medical office insurance staff members deal with daily force them to develop both proactive and reactive coping strategies. They construct a way of understanding the intricacies of their job by paying attention to and linking cues and looking retrospectively at events to interpret and create consistencies. Medical office insurance staff members develop personal characteristics, place emphasis on experience, and depend on effective communication skills to lessen the frustration and deal with their work situations.

Responsible

"I do whatever needs to be done."

Medical office insurance staff members prove to be responsible actors on behalf of the interests of organizations, patients, and regulations. Insurance staff members view their primary role in the organization as getting the claim paid to "get the money in the door." They identify with the financial responsibility of the organization and take personal responsibility to work the claims, create and work error lists, research accounts, and understand and fix rejections. When medical office insurance staff members discuss the work they do, they often make references to charges, payments, denials, and collections. Most of the actions of medical office insurance staff center on resolving accounts to bring revenue into the medical practice. Insurance staff members know that it is their job to "to get that claim paid," and they add with pride, "I do whatever needs to be done."

Beyond financial responsibility, medical office insurance staff members take on the responsibility of oversight of their organizations. Often insurance staff members will jump rank when necessary to clarify and implement a new Medicare rule that management may not have handled properly. They know that, as a representative of the office, and knowing about the effective date of the new rule, implementation "is still my responsibility" even if management has not acted. Insurance staff understands that the organization should "not take a chance on filing erroneous claims," and they understand that whatever is done wrong "is always going to fall on the clinic." Expressions of insurance staff members reflect concern for the well-being of their organization. This financial and oversight responsibility for the organization engenders the willingness of medical office insurance staff members to act with autonomy and make interpretations and respond on behalf of the organization. This sensemaking behavior gives individuals meaning and a sense of place in the organization.

Medical office insurance staff members are closely linked with the organization. It is the organizational structure that helps make sense of external events and translates cues so that self-identity is not shaken. They have high motivation to preserve and protect the good image of the organization. By doing so, individuals enhance their own self-image and confirm their identity in the organization.

In addition, insurance staff members are quite conscious of their responsibility for the individual patients they serve. Often this fiduciary responsibility seems to be assumed without directive from the organization for which they work. Medical office insurance staff members clearly play a role in educating their patient clients as noted when they refer to calling patients to explain situations "as best they can." Staff members accept responsibility and take the opportunity to assist patients. They help patients when they believe patients are deserving but show no inclination to help if they perceive the patient may be involved in a dishonest scheme. They accept responsibility to act, but their help is based on the circumstances of each situation.

Persistent

> "I will keep pursuing it, and I won't drop it at all."

Medical office insurance staff members prove to be persistent as they pursue their work. Staff members often speak of situations when "research" is necessary, and they talk about how they "have to gather information" before problems can be resolved. They talk about how they spend "all day long trying to figure out why a claim did not get paid," which exemplifies the determination with which they approach their work. They also refer repeatedly to the difficulty of getting accurate information; they use phrases to describe their effort such as, "I will keep pursuing it and I won't drop it at all" and "I...try and spot-check problems." Staff members report that "every claim I work is something different," and that they have to "figure out" what the situation is and spend a lot of time "solving problems."

The complexity of their work is apparent in reports such as, "it probably took two hours out of my day to straighten this mess out." The diligence necessary to straighten out problems sometimes involves "twenty questions"; "call, call, and call again"; "fix and re-fix"; and "file and refile." Regardless, resolving issues and ensuring that issues are not created requires concentration from medical office insurance staff members as they do their work: "I look at each super-bill [charge ticket], and not only am I keying in numbers, I also look at what insurance it is, and what else has been checked on the super-bill to make sure it all goes together."

Working denials requires a great deal of research and concentration. "If something abnormal comes up...it is my job to handle it." Although working denials or rejections is outside of the standard insurance filling process, medical office insurance staff members regularly speak of "working denials" as they discuss the non-routine work they do. The frequency with which denials are discussed implies the irony that denials are, in fact, a routine part of the insurance process.

Undoubtedly, working each denied claim is different and, therefore, is a part of the non-routine work of the medical office insurance staff. The obligation that medical office insurance staff members feel to their organization "to get the claim paid" necessitates perseverance. "One day, I spent probably three hours, being batted from one place to another." For this reason managers should understand that measuring goal performance is difficult. The unpredictable nature of the work done by the medical office insurance staff encourages persistence in problem solving, and the best staff members show perseverance in doing their work even when the amount of time is lengthy.

Self-Reliant

> "I work pretty independently."

Medical office insurance staff members exhibit the ability to work independently and use the resources at their disposal to resolve questions. Insurance staff members report that they "have to make a lot of decisions" and that they "work pretty independently." They reflect their self-sufficient attitude in saying, "I like to direct myself. I know what I need to do and I do it." In addition, their conversation about their work reflects their independence: "If I get fed up...I will switch to something else"; "I work it throughout the week"; "I make my own schedule"; and "what I do in a day will just depend on what comes on my plate during the day...sometimes I have to jump from one thing to another." Without hesitancy they "write up a charge correction sheet" when something is billed incorrectly. Medical office insurance staff members, without reluctance, call Medicare, request to speak with a higher Medicare authority if necessary, train coworkers, fix denials, change codes, refuse to change codes, help clients, decline to help clients, implement policy, and more. All this is done regularly without direction from management and with little physician contact.

While remaining mindful of rules and regulations, medical office insurance staff members work according to their own judgment; they create boundaries for themselves and exercise autonomy according to their own preferences. Medical office insurance staff members do what is reasonable with the hope that their action is also accurate. They exercise a high degree of discretion and maximize autonomy.

This behavior is attributed in part to their complicated work. Their work is too complicated to be prescriptive, and the volume of work is too great for close supervision. Although the complex nature of their work requires judgment calls to be made, medical office insurance staff members generally do not seek supervision. Their tendency toward self-reliant behavior points out that they might be reluctant to accept close supervision if permitted or prescribed methods are offered. Staff members concur with each other, "you try to get as much stuff done and over with as possible"; "we have to get into it and figure it out"; and "I feel like every patient account, every claim I work, is something different. That is what I like about working insurance." These expressions verify that medical office insurance staff members are self-reliant in working without close supervision or prescribed methods. They decide "what is wrong and in what directions the situation needs to be changed."

Place Emphasis on Experience

"What I usually do in that situation..."

Medical office insurance staff members place emphasis on experience as a strategy for dealing with the complex nature of their work. They often rely on knowledge from past jobs they have had both in and out of health care. Even though they are confronted with a large volume of complex and technical information, medical office insurance staff members have little or no formal training to do their work. Typically, they have not completed an intensive, lengthy, and rigorous course of education and training like their organization's physicians. Rather, these staff members have obtained their skills and knowledge from on-the-job training. Their learning together in the organization has benefited both the individual and the organization. As they learn from experience, they affect the organization and, likewise, the organization affects them both personally and in the way they carry out the duties of their work.

As they recount their job experiences in health care, the breadth of their work experience is clear. Staff members express no sense that they were not adequately trained to handle their work or that they were deficient in any way to do their work. Rather, they speak with pride about their ability to do the "whole thing." They assert, "I do multiple things"; "I do a little bit of everything"; and "I just do a lot of different things." Their personal confidence implies that they can "fix anything that is not right" or handle "basically anything that anyone throws at me." This confidence is a result of having performed many job duties and worked in many contexts in the health care industry.

Undoubtedly, these medical office insurance staff members demonstrate that they have specialized knowledge that both the physicians they work for and the patients they serve are not privy to. Without formalized training, these staff members have successfully made sense of what is going on around them as they assess their experiences from the various jobs and apply that experience to retain a position in health care that is critical to the financial well-being of their medical practice.

Effective Communicators

"It is asking the right person the right question."

Effective communication is an essential element in carrying out the work of medical office insurance staff. The occasions for communication are constant. Staff members communicate with business office coworkers, clinical staff such as physicians and nurses, representatives from governmental and commercial insurance carriers, and patients and their representatives. The act of effective communication requires both giving and receiving information. Therefore, medical office insurance staff must have good verbal communication skills.

Technical and analytical skills are also necessary for effective communication. For example, staff members speak of the importance of getting information on the Internet. The technical skill to use the Internet enhances the ability to gain input. The analytical skill of knowing who to talk to, where to gain necessary information, what information is valid, when to act on information, and how to impart information is essential to work effectively and efficiently. Medical office insurance staff members are engaged in the process of determining which variables are reasonable, and, as they work, they depend on communication to resolve situations.

The telephone is the dominant method of verbal communication. In fact, phone calls consume the work life of many medical office insurance staff members. Staff relates, "I talk to patients that have called or I call the patient for something or I call Medicare to ask a question." Staff reports that they "make phone calls to insurance companies" to get information or straighten out a misunderstanding. "Everything we do requires calling the insurance carrier." These calls to insurance carriers often result in the staff feeling as if they get the run around. For example, staff members report, "it is always, well, you need to call this number" and of course, that number is different from the one they just called. Again, medical office insurance staff members use the telephone as they seek by trial and error to establish a stable process.

Medicare seems to be first on the call list when staff members are in doubt about how to handle a situation. Staff members typically comment, "I would call Medicare," or "you might end up calling Medicare." It should be noted that often more than one time-consuming phone call is required to resolve an insurance situation. Medical office insurance staff members try to make sense of their work by calling Medicare. Sometimes they rely on trial and error; they see what will work and what won't, or they see what Medicare tells them in two out of three calls.

Patient calls can also be time-consuming. Staff reports, "I call them back one at a time...I return all their calls, answer their questions the best that I can." Staff members indicate that more telephone time is spent giving patients explanations than getting information from them. Regardless, staff members concur, that there are "a lot of phone calls involved" in the work they do.

Medical office insurance staff members also realize the importance of perfecting the art of asking questions whether on the phone or in person. To get essential information they must "...ask the right person the right question." They advise that the right question can clear up a situation that has been ongoing for months. Communication with in-house staff is also critical. Staff members remark on the necessity of getting the right diagnosis and correctly matching diagnosis and procedure. They report that "sometimes the doctors and nurses just do not realize how important it is to get a diagnosis that will work with that particular procedure." They also report the necessity of getting the correct date of injury, and the general necessity of having important facts at hand for reference.

Medical office insurance staff members made very few references to speaking with physicians directly. They want to ensure that documentation matches what is charged, and, when it doesn't, they suggest that they would leave a note for the physician explaining what needed to be done. This points to an ironic situation. The behavior of medical office insurance staff indicates clearly that they assume financial responsibility for the organizations. Yet it is physicians who render services that generate revenue. The lack of regular and direct communication with physicians seems like disconnected behavior. Although staff engages in conversation with all parties — business office coworkers, clinical staff, insurance carriers' representatives, and patients and their representatives — insurance staff members do not speak regularly with physicians, perhaps out of respect for physicians' time or because of their own time constraints. To acquire the information they need, in the absence of regular and open communication, staff members must be resourceful, paying attention to small cues and creating linkages where opportunities arise.

MAJOR TENSIONS CONFRONTED BY MEDICAL OFFICE INSURANCE STAFF

Medical office insurance staff members confront two major tensions in the course of doing their work. The first tension is between independent and dependent behaviors of medical office insurance staff members. The second tension is between patient-focused and organization-focused behaviors. On one end of a spectrum are the patients' needs, and on the other, are the organization's needs. The organization may include the physician's practice, the insurance carriers, and government-mandated regulations.

Before we discuss the major tensions confronted by the medical office insurance staff, it is beneficial to explore the perceptions, attitudes, beliefs, and actions of the medical office insurance staff members so that we can gain insight into how they resolve these tensions.

Perceptions of Medical Office Insurance Staff Members

Perceptions reflect conscious recognitions. Medical office insurance staff members perceive that they share a social context with their co-workers, but that they also act individually as they make sense of their work. They also know that their work is important. They make statements such as, "I am given a work file of all the denials and I know it is up to me to figure them out," and "I know what I have to do and I do it." The perceptions of staff members are transferred to clients, who seem to realize that staff members can make their life better or worse.

That insurance staff members share a social context in their own group and in the larger organization is evidenced by comments about the work they share in common and the experiences they share from on-the-job-training: "surprise, surprise, they do it all the time" and "that has happened to me many times." That staff members are self-conscious sensemakers can be heard in their descriptions of the manner in which they "try to avoid" situations that will defeat their purpose of getting reimbursed for the claims they submit: in order to get paid they "concentrate"; "watch and make sure"; and "correct whatever needs to be done." Staff members perceive their work as important; they "check everything," and make sure that situations are "taken care of properly."

The volume and complexity of their work produce such matter-of-fact statements as "there is too much information for anyone to know everything." They contend with misinformation from patients, mistakes from physicians and coworkers, inconsistency from insurance carriers, and a myriad of unclear rules and regulations from Medicare. Still rationality prevails. They see the things they can do something about. When they perceive that they cannot do anything effective about what is happening they tend to focus on the information they can do something about.

Attitudes of Medical Office Insurance Staff Members

The attitudes of medical office insurance staff members affect staff members' quality of thinking and are capable of improving the chances for wise or appropriate actions. For example, when goal expectations are ambiguous, vague, or conflicting, staff members may feel that these conditions are inherent in their jobs and that, in order to do their jobs, it is necessary to pay attention to a wide variety of inputs. Often they simply accept that whatever they see, they will figure out some way to cope with it. Their attitude is that they are capable of doing many things effectively: "I do whatever needs to be done… it is my job to get the claim paid." They accept that they will need to make numerous significant decisions, and they hope that they will have the experience to make those decisions: "I go in and either call the insurance carrier or I re-file the claim, whatever I feel is the best way to handle it." Medical office insurance staff members oppose dealing with inadequate resources but seem to realize that they cannot get ahead of the demand for services: "The underlying issue is that there is not any help coming." Also, they often share the attitude that it is a part of their role to support, assist, and educate clients. They consider helping as "a part of their job."

Medical office insurance staff members rarely defer to management for answers on how to handle situations; rather they use their experience-based discretion to solve problems. Medical office insurance staff members recognize the consequences of the lack of adequate resources, such as experienced front office staff: "They are not paid enough to keep them in order to learn and really get into doing their jobs right." Even though medical office insurance staff members identify inadequate resources as a "major problem," they are pragmatic enough to "realize that it is never all going to get done. You can do what you can."

Medical office insurance staff members often provide assistance to patients in the form of answering questions and educating them on everything from their office visit to the insurance claims process so that patients are better able to help themselves. Insurance staff members share the attitude that it is their role to be supportive of patient-clients in dealing with their access to services.

Beliefs of Medical Office Insurance Staff Members

Many medical office insurance staff members believe that it is reasonable to use general problem-solving and decision-making skills to deal with the situations they face and that each situation should be assessed based on the individual circumstances of that situation. In addition, staff members largely believe their work to be non-routine. Even when staff members respond that their work is routine, they often describe the work they do as being anything but the monotony that might normally be associated with routine work. The statement by a staff member clarifies the idea of routine versus non-routine work: "I feel like every patient account, every claim I work is something different." In other words, it is routine to work claims, but each claim presents different issues that are not routine.

Many medical office insurance staff members believe that, too often, rules are unclear. As a result, sometimes staff members give conflicting information because of misunderstanding, sometimes they revert to consensus of opinion, and sometimes they apply general problem-solving skills. Sometimes they even seek the opinion of a higher authority — Medicare. Medical office insurance staff members often ask for written documentation to clarify the intent of the rules. All of these methods represent logical courses of action.

Medical office insurance staff members regularly and comfortably exercise discretion. Discretion is in the comfort zone of insurance staff members and indicates that they and their management consider discretion to be legitimate. In addition, medical office insurance staff members indicate that they believe they have a fiduciary responsibility to the patient-clients they serve.

Only a few medical office insurance staff members hesitate to make a full complement of decisions. For example, when Medicare was not recognizing a new code, staff responded by saying, "I would probably turn this over to the coding supervisor" and "I would not attempt to do anything about coding without sending it through the supervisor." Another says, "I would talk to the office manager and explain the situation and get clarification from her on what she wanted us to do." Those medical office insurance staff members act more like bureaucrats and do not believe it is their role to resolve issues. Those staff members believe that management should resolve issues because discretion is not legitimate. While this belief is an exception, managers should be on the lookout for insurance personnel who don't exercise discretion and who do not accept fiduciary responsibility.

Actions of Medical Office Insurance Staff Members

To reiterate the actions of street-level bureaucrats, medical office insurance staff members often operate independently without direct supervision in organizations. This independent action may be accepted because of the lack of structure within organizations. Their independence is allowed or granted in part because the tasks they engage in are not routine. The work environment requires individuals whose actions are adaptable, flexible, and resourceful. Often medical office insurance staff members express their adaptability, flexibility, and resourcefulness like this: "There is not a typical day. I put out fires and it depends on the day." Because their work lacks prescribed formats, actions of the medical office insurance staff must include decision making.

Medical office insurance staff members function within a set of values drawn from their perceptions, attitudes, and beliefs. They assess the circumstances of a situation and draw on the values and norms that they are familiar with to direct their actions about what to do and how to do it. They may act without full knowledge of the situation they are in so they use the information they have and personal judgment to guide their decision making about which actions to take. They strive for coherent behavior that is directed by their memory of past events. Their action produces meaning of their world and encourages further continuous action. For example, medical office insurance staff members may make a telephone call when they are unsure how to deal with an issue at hand. Whether they call the insurance company or Medicare's coordination of benefits department, they hope to get information that will provide understanding that will direct further action.

Medical office insurance staff members make choices after assessing alternatives in light of memories of past events because of their own stake in the situation and their responsibility to either the organization or to the patient-clients they serve. "If Medicare says it is going to be implemented then you probably need to go with it." Medical office insurance staff members display their willingness to act without seeking input from management, although their action is not without consideration of the organization's best interest.

Tension between Independent and Dependent Behavior

The perceptions, attitudes, beliefs, and actions typical of street-level bureaucrats typically dominate the behavior of medical office insurance staff. Although some behavior is consistent with that of bureaucratic behavior, the nature of the work of the medical office insurance staff — its high volume and complexity — requires independent action in order for staff members to manage the job on an on-going basis. Too much dependency on management would create a backlog of work. The advice of one insurance staff member sums it up by saying that, "we have to realize that it is never all going to get done. We do what we can while we are here, and we hope to get to all of it, and that's all we can do."

Non-routine work, such as working denials, is often mentioned when medical office insurance staff members discuss what occurs in a typical day. Work at this end of the spectrum is characterized by ambiguity. Staff must engage in sensemaking to resolve non-routine work and in doing so they exercise discretion based on experience. Medical office insurance staff members demonstrate that they use past experience when they report that they seek "written confirmation" and "call Medicare" without input from management; when they note that the physician needs "to put an addendum in the chart"; when they interpret Centers for Medicare & Medicaid Services (CMS) guidelines; and when they work with fellow staff members to "make them responsible for... getting correct information." These actions occur independently without deferring to management for solutions.

At the other, dependent end of the spectrum, medical office insurance staff members do routine work in a clearly prescribed fashion and make repetitive decisions that have been programmed by organizational processes. Staff members must follow the organizational rules and defer any non-routine decision making to a superior in the organization. For example, if the implementation date for a new Medicare rule occurs while the manager is out of the office, bureaucratic staff members would make no attempt to implement the rule because they would not consider that they had the authority to take on that organizational role.

The tension that medical office insurance staff members feel between acting with dependent behavior and acting with independent behavior is primarily resolved because of the necessity to solve problems to facilitate the processing of work. They see their work as getting payment for the practice. They say "we get the money in the door." They consider most of their work as non-routine because it does not lend itself to a straightforward course of action. Much of their work consists of working denials that must be approached with the tenacity of a detective. Therefore, most medical office insurance staff members act independently. They act their way into a clearer understanding of their work and their role in the organization.

Tension between Patient and Organizational Needs

The second major tension faced by medical office insurance staff is between serving the needs of the patient and serving the needs of the organization. Medical office insurance staff members often experience conflict in deciding whether to concentrate their efforts on serving the patient's or the organization's needs. When serving the organization's needs, staff may be engaged on behalf of the physician's organization, the commercial insurance organization, or the governmental insurance organization of Medicare. In some situations more than one of these organizations may have needs to be served simultaneously. Sometimes medical office insurance staff members are faced with situations where the needs of both the patient and the organization cannot be fully served. Thus, tension arises around whose needs should be most satisfied.

The majority of medical office insurance staff members claim the discretion to choose, when necessary, whether to honor the needs of the patient or to act in the best interest of the organization. The choice is reflected in their behavior. Clearly, there are examples when medical office staff will serve the needs of the organization. More pertinent is to understand how medical office insurance staff members use discretion to define and solve problems when situations are presented that involve serving both the patient and the organization.

Medical office insurance staff members understand that they are confronted with situations that are not in their realm of oversight. In these situations they may ask themselves "whose problem is it?" to resolve the situation. Generally when confronted with problems, staff members do not readily take on problems that do not rightfully belong to them. For example, if a problem falls within the physician's domain, such as inadequate documentation for the charge level indicated, they consider it the physician's duty to take care of the problem. In this example, medical office insurance staff members will not hesitate to send the charge back to the doctor for the necessary information, and advise that the dictation would have to be amended if the doctor chose to keep the charge level. Most staff members, after identifying the problem that the dictation and charge are not compatible, leave the correction of the problem to the physician. Likewise, if the situation is to provide proof of insurance coverage for insurance billing, they consider it the patient's responsibility to provide that information. Both of these examples are evidence that medical office insurance staff members use discretion to set the boundaries that direct their behavior in dealing with situations like these.

Staff members are more likely to intervene on behalf of the patient before they will intervene on behalf of the physicians who employ them. They may choose to direct a patient even when they know that the ultimate resolution to the problem depends on the patient. However, the degree of responsibility that staff members are willing to accept on the patient's behalf differs, and their approaches to help may be diverse. The comparison of these situations points out that medical office insurance staff members feel a fiduciary responsibility to educate patients and support their needs to a greater degree than they feel toward the physicians for whom they work. One staff member clearly stated her position in saying, "I think that nowadays the doctors have to be responsible for what they dictate. They know it is their business. If you are running a business you have to know those kinds of things, so it is their responsibility."

Generally staff members as a group show more empathy for the patient's situation. Often staff members will take an active role to help and make comments that show their willingness for involvement, such as "so she would need to get information for him." When situations deal with the frustrating "whose problem is it" question, staff members choose to define their role in each problem differently, and their evaluations of the alternatives leading to action are not parallel. Staff members use discretion based on attitude, belief, and past experience to resolve their roles and responsibilities in these non-routine work situations.

When staff members are presented with a request from a patient to help choose an insurance policy that would supplement Medicare Part B insurance, staff overwhelmingly agreed to assist in getting information to help the patient make the decision, but will typically stop short of making the decision for the patient. Staff members say that they definitely do not want to tell the patient which coverage to take because the patient could come back and say, "you told me to get this one and it is not a good insurance." Here the staff member's concern over her limits and the liability of both herself and her organization kept her from fulfilling the patient's request.

Staff members may also try to mitigate the liability for both themselves and the organization and satisfy the patient's request. "I think she could be free to say, 'I can't tell you which is better but I can tell you that this is good,' or 'my dad has this one or this person has this one' without mentioning names and that 'they typically pay pretty quickly.'" The staff member would, by inference, give a specific insurance name and advocate based on her father's experience with it. The staff member went on to say, "I would really feel comfortable doing that myself and as a matter of fact I have done that in the past." This staff member values the role of supporting patients so much that it dictates her behavior.

Another staff member tried to balance serving both the patient and the organization. This staff person would "not pick for her" but would help the patient "get a list" of possible insurance plans. The staff member also said, "I would try to get the information for her," such as "phone numbers so she may call them."

Responses like this indicate that medical office insurance staff members also keep the concerns of the organization —their physician's organization, commercial insurance, and Medicare — in mind when helping out patients. Both commercial insurance and Medicare would expect medical office insurance staff members to be neutral about which insurance plan a patient should seek. Even Medicare does not make recommendations to their beneficiaries about which supplemental insurance policy to purchase. Instead, Medicare provides a list. As such, Medicare would expect the same from medical office insurance staff. Commercial insurance carriers rely on the fact that licenses are issued to sell insurance and would not expect prejudicial recommendations to come from medical office insurance staff. As one staff member pointed out, insurance staff members — because of liability — cannot make an explicit directive. Advice that might come back to haunt the physician's organization cannot be given.

In situations in which patients ask medical office insurance staff members to help understand medical bills, even though none of the bills relate to the organization that employs them, most staff members will agree to help the patient because the individual is a patient of the physician organization that employs them. The tension that exists is between spending time helping the patient and spending time working to provide a direct benefit to the physician organization. Most staff members accept a fiduciary role that is common in professionals. They feel a responsibility to the patient and are likely to help the patient on the organization's time. They allow their sense of responsibility to the patient to outweigh the responsibility they feel to their organization.

Some staff members feel their responsibility to be equal. Those who feel this equal responsibility strongly will help the patient on their own time. They may help the patient before work hours, during lunch, or after work hours. Only a few staff members have such strong organizational concerns that they will choose to limit help to patients. Rather, they refer the patient to the organization where the services on the bill were provided. These staff members worry about complying with boundaries. Some boundaries are self-imposed, such as time constraints imposed by office work that needs to be completed. Other boundaries, like the Health Insurance Portability and Accountability Act (HIPAA) rule relating to patient privacy and confidentiality, are externally imposed.

When presented with a situation in which a patient asks a medical office insurance staff member to participate in a dishonest scheme, staff members show little tolerance for intentional dishonesty. Although this situation gives rise to an opportunity for divided loyalty between patient and organization, insurance staff members usually do not have a problem acting on behalf of the organizations involved. They have sufficient education, training, and experience to be vigilant in spotting fraud. They seem to be indignant that a patient would try to involve them in such a scheme and are adamant that dishonesty will be detrimental to someone — Medicare, employer, insurance carrier, or their organization. Their lack of tolerance for dishonesty has more to do with intrinsic values and less to do with Medicare's fraud and abuse initiative. Their reaction seems to stem from personal pride of place within the health care industry.

Medical office insurance staff members tend to resolve the tension between patients' needs and the organization's needs based on the circumstances of the situation. When they consider the circumstantial factors of the situation, staff members draw on values that are based on their attitudes and beliefs rooted in past experience. Medical office insurance staff members feel an obligation to and responsibility for both patients and organizations. As they consider factors, they weigh consequences of behavior based on their own stake, the patient's stake, and the organization's stake in the situation. Medical office insurance staff members are most comfortable when they can act independently and focus on the patient's needs. Although it may appear that medical insurance office staff members subject the Medicare program to vulnerability, in actuality insurance staff members seem to offer the best likelihood that Medicare beneficiaries will be served according to their individual needs.

INFLUENCES IN MEDICARE IMPLEMENTATION

Medical office insurance staff members regularly make decisions using general problem-solving processes in the context of the circumstance at hand. Their influence in completing the essential functions of a medical office is illustrated by the way in which the styles of non-street-level bureaucrats and street-level bureaucrats play out in medical office insurance departments in the areas of decision making and service delivery.

Decision Making

Bureaucrats expect and want top management to make decisions. They want decisions to be handed down in a formal manner, and they expect all decisions to be binding. They take comfort in knowing that decisions are made systematically on knowledge greater than they possess and that they will have occasion for routine processes where repetitive decision making is in order. Decisions in their organizations are highly controlled, and they would never presume to use the discretion to make a decision that was outside of standard operating procedure for their routine tasks.

On the other hand, street-level bureaucrats, serving as a model for medical office insurance staff members, are not so confined. They make decisions based on a range of circumstantial factors using general problem-solving processes — they define a problem, identify and evaluate alternatives, make a decision, and act on the decision. Street-level bureaucrats have a stake in their decisions and their outcomes because they have a stake in the organizations for which they work and in the patient-clients they serve.

Service Delivery

A bureaucrat delivers services in the medical office equally without regard to individual needs. A bureaucratic staff member refuses to give any information about how to purchase the best Medicare supplemental insurance policy, does not even consider helping a patient sort out bills, and does not feel any personal passion about a patient's dishonest scheme.

On the other hand, medical office insurance staff members (street-level bureaucrats) insert themselves in every situation to some degree. Street-level medical office insurance staff members get involved because they tend to feel personal involvement with their patient-clients. They realize how complicated medical insurance is and how difficult it can be to access the Medicare system for services. They volunteer to help sort out a patient's bills because they know "how tangled" it can be after an illness involving many services from many different providers.

Medical office insurance staff members also prove to be compassionate. Bureaucratic model staff members do not allow any personal feelings or sentiments to creep into the process of service delivery. Rather, they assess their duty in the situation and act on duty only. They do not allow personal opinions or attitudes to influence their actions. Street-level staff members, on the other hand, allow their attitudes to influence their actions. They counsel and support patients and they educate patients about how the health care insurance system works. Street-level staff members do not worry about strict application of the rules because they believe that discretion is a necessary and legitimate part of service delivery. Strictly bureaucratic staff disapproves of the use of discretion and strictly avoids any situations that might call for discretion.

The way in which medical office insurance staff members — street-level bureaucrats — engage in service delivery is different than how a bureaucrat delivers service. For example, if bureaucrats found themselves in a position in which a new Medicare rule was to go into effect before management gave a directive on how to implement the change, the bureaucrats would not implement the change. They would not alter their application of service delivery to accommodate the change unless management had given a highly prescriptive formula for dealing with the change. They would expect management to control the implementation of the new rule by composing memos and standardized forms, and compiling policy manuals describing how the new change would be standardized. Only when standard operating procedure was clear would the bureaucrats engage in the new task and delivery of the new service could occur. While waiting for management, bureaucrats would not work the front desk for a co-worker who was sick, they would not fill in for the cashier, and they would not devise creative ways to get information as the medical office insurance staff members of this study did because they practice strict division of labor. If it is not their job, they would not do it, nor would they feel any obligation that they should do it. They would not "dig and dig," and "go through charts and look for something else to see if there is anything else we can do" in order to "get the claim paid" and "get the money in the door." Bureaucrats feel as separate from the organization for which they work as they are from the individuals accessing the services they deliver. They do not recognize individual needs.

MEDICAL OFFICE INSURANCE STAFF: AN EMERGING PROFESSION

Medical office insurance staff members have intrinsic conflicting goals. On the one hand, they try to maximize reimbursement for the organization. On the other hand, they operate within a set of complex rules with inadequate resources. All the while, they try to serve the patient-client who depends on them. The study of medical office insurance staff members suggests that their work is an emerging profession that is in need of structured training and certification.

Managers must recognize the difficulty of the work environment of the medical office insurance staff and help employees merge competing interests by providing useful training and education. To support adequate training, managers need to acquaint themselves with the principles of training employees. In addition, when assessing the job requirements of employees, managers would serve their organizations well to use evaluation tools designed to reflect the employee's ability to adapt to change. Further, individuals need to be assessed based on employee characteristics, such as motivation to learn, that indicate an individual's willingness to adapt to change.

In addition to understanding training principles, managers need to become versed in the levels of learning so that they can assess what tasks employees are ready to perform in accordance with the organization's objectives. Managers need to take the responsibility to assess the learning and skill levels involved with specific tasks so that the appropriate level of learning, moving from rote learning at the lowest level to applying learned skills at the highest level, can be optimized in hiring practices. Understanding and matching employees' skills and abilities with tasks will be beneficial to both managers and organizations.

Organizations would be well served to make hiring decisions based on an individual's propensity to use good decision-making skills. Managers are charged with the responsibility to evaluate potential employees' approach to problem solving. They must determine potential employees' ability to define a problem, reevaluate the situation, gather more information if needed, consider all solutions, think of alternatives, choose the best alternative, and act on the resulting decision. Employees who have a disciplined approach to decision making will be able to serve the organization's goals better if the organization establishes a culture of shared meaning for the employee to draw from when solving problems.

Finally, managers need to recognize and understand the complexity of the work undertaken by medical office insurance staff and encourage staff members to think and behave as professionals. The Medicare "rule book" is larger than the United States Internal Revenue Service code. Yet, those in our society who interpret the IRS tax code are professionals who act with autonomy, have a fiduciary responsibility to the clients they serve, and master a large body of specialized knowledge. Medical office insurance staff members also act with autonomy, have a fiduciary responsibility to clients, and have mastery of a large body of specialized knowledge. They too need to be trained, educated, and certified as medical office insurance staff specialists. The study of medical office insurance staff members suggests that their work is an emerging profession that is in need of structured training and certification.

References

1. Holt, S. J. "Street-Level Implementation of Medicare Policy: Exploring the Role of Medical Office Insurance Staff." 2004. A dissertation presented to the Faculty of the Graduate School of Saint Louis University.

2. Lipsky, M. *Street-Level Bureaucracy.* (New York: Russell Sage, 1980): 28.

3. Weick, K.E. *Sensemaking in Organizations.* (Thousand Oaks, CA: Sage Publications, 1980): 87.

CHAPTER THREE

Elements of Billing and Payment

The ultimate goal of the billing process is reimbursement. For the reimbursement process from insurance carriers to work correctly, several conditions must be met at distinct junctures in the billing process. And at each juncture is the opportunity for ambiguity for medical office insurance staff members. Much of the uncertainty exists because of complex and confusing sets of regulations that do not exist in isolation, but are compounded by a lengthy programmatic attempt on the part of the Centers for Medicare & Medicaid Services (CMS) to control the cost and rate of growth in health care. A review of the items that determine the charge value of services and procedures will set the stage for an understanding of the health care billing and payment process.

CURRENT PROCEDURAL TERMINOLOGY

The Current Procedural Terminology (CPT)* code set is the official standard system of codes established by the American Medical Association (AMA) for the medical industry. The CPT code set consists of five-digit codes coupled with descriptive terms used to describe each medical service and procedure providers may deliver to patients. The purpose of CPT codes is to provide uniformity across the medical spectrum of care — medical, surgical, and diagnostic services. It is intended to be used broadly by all health care entities so that there can be no misunderstanding of what services were provided.

CPT codes are designed to pay for physician services — both procedures and Evaluation and Management (E/M) services. The directive is to use the CPT code that most closely describes the service or procedure that was provided to the patient. CPT codes are not intended to approximate the service but to exactly describe the service. (*Note:* As long as physician collaboration exists and general supervising rules are followed, Medicare will pay for E/M services provided by a physician assistant [PA], nurse practitioner [NP], clinical nurse specialist [CNS], or certified nurse midwife [CNM]. Payment is determined by medical necessity of the service combined with billing under the appropriate

*CPT©2009 American Medical Association. All rights reserved.

individual CPT code requirements.) When a new service or procedure is developed and a CPT code does not exist for that service or procedure, the AMA invites medical professionals to request that a new descriptive code be developed. (Request forms to use for suggestions may be found at www.ama-assn.org/ama/pub/category/3866.html.)

The AMA maintains the CPT code set yearly. While the CPT code set predated the Health Insurance Portability and Accountability Act (HIPAA), HIPAA mandates the use of CPT codes when filing all electronic transactions for financial reimbursement. The CPT codebook, published annually by the AMA, begins with complete instructions for using CPT codes. The book is divided into six sections — E/M, Anesthesia, Surgery, Radiology, Pathology and Laboratory, and Medicine — and holds a wealth of knowledge about the medical coding process.

Although managers may consider the CPT codebook to serve primarily as a resource for coders, it also is an indispensable resource for insurance staff members. Organizations should provide easy access to current CPT codebooks for insurance department staff members to use when working insurance claims. If insurance staff members have access to updated books and feel comfortable using and making notations in the book, they will work claims more efficiently with less guesswork and mystery.

INTERNATIONAL CLASSIFICATION OF DISEASES, NINTH REVISION

The World Health Organization maintains the International Classification of Diseases (ICD) to track and classify morbidity and mortality for statistical purposes across the globe. *ICD-9* refers to the *International Classification of Diseases, Ninth Revision*. While the most recent version is ICD-10, that version has not been well received for use in the United States. Rather, ICD-9-CM is used in the United States and is compatible with the parent system, ICD-9. *CM* stands for *Clinical Modification*, and ICD-9-CM has been designated by CMS as the coding system to be used by physicians when billing for services.

The ICD-9-CM code set, coupled with the CPT code set, describes precisely the clinical picture of the patient. ICD-9-CM expands on ICD-9 by using a fifth-digit to allow for a greater level of detail or specificity that is retained in the medical record for better tracking purposes. ICD-9 uses a three-digit rubric that is adequate for statistical purposes at an international level to classify manifestations of disease but is not precise enough to describe medical necessity of a procedure.

Like the CPT codebook, the ICD-9-CM codebook (published by various book publishers) is a valuable resource for individuals working in the insurance department to find information about a diagnosis, condition, or disease. The ICD-9-CM codebook lays out the following 10-step plan for correct coding:

1. Describe the reason for the visit. Do not code based on uncertainty (that is, suspected or probable conditions).
2. Use Volume 2, the Alphabetic Index, first before the Tabular List.

3. Find the main entry term in the Alphabetic Index that is arranged by condition.

4. Review and interpret italicized notes listed with the main term.

5. Review modifiers.

6. Pay attention to cross-references, abbreviations, and brackets.

7. After choosing a tentative code, locate it in the tabular list.

8. Determine the highest level of specificity — assign a five-digit code if possible.

9. Use the key at the bottom of the page for definitions of colors and symbols.

10. Assign the code.

Like CPT codes, ICD-9-CM codes are revised annually, and medical practices should accommodate staff by purchasing new books to optimize efficiency.

RELATIVE VALUE UNIT

A relative value unit (RVU) is a standardized collective value assigned to a procedure or service for reimbursement purposes. An RVU is a term that comes from the Resource-Based Relative Value Scale (RBRVS) payment schedule, which is a national uniform system used for reimbursing all physician services that went into effect in 1992. The intent of RBRVS was to create consistent payment policies for physician reimbursement that is equitable to physicians all over the United States. Prior to RBRVS, physician reimbursement was based on actual, customary, and prevailing charges; there was little rhyme or reason to physicians' reimbursement schedules, and costs continued to rise significantly each year with no end in sight.

CMS, with the clear understanding that reimbursement for health care services is a complex process, shaped the RBRVS system to establish, as accurately as possible, a cost base for the skill, time, and resources involved in every physician service provided to patients — both procedures and E/M services. CMS's use of RBRVS ensures that the agency can prudently purchase health care services for its beneficiaries. Further, the establishment of RBRVS ensured that CMS could achieve the objective of statutory requirements to control costs in Medicare for physician reimbursement under the sustainable growth rate (SGR) mandates.

The case can be made that RBRVS is similar to the time and motion studies used in the industry sector since the Industrial Revolution's outgrowth of the assembly line. RBRVS has, without question, been revolutionary in changing physicians' reimbursement. Three major factors are used to calculate fees using RBRVS:

- Relative value units (RVUs);
- Geographic practice cost indices (GPCIs); and
- The conversion factor (CF).

CMS, as required by law, uses these three factors to calculate physician fees or payment amounts annually under the RBRVS system.

RVU, the first major factor, is divided into three components that are defined in the CPT codebook — work, practice expense, and malpractice expense. The first of these components, work (RVUw), reflects the physician's "resources of skill, time, and intensity of effort to furnish the service." Procedures and services with higher RVUs produce higher reimbursement for physicians. The second component, practice expense (RVUpe), represents "the overhead expenses incurred to provide the space, equipment, supplies, and support personnel cost for providing the services." The third component, malpractice expense (RVUm), represents the impact each procedure or service has on the cost of professional liability insurance paid by the physician.

The second factor of RBRVS is the GPCI. The GPCI varies by region and compares each region to a national average. There may be several regions per state. A GPCI for each region is established for each of the RVU elements — work, practice expense, and malpractice. Each of the established GPCIs is multiplied by its corresponding RVU element value to help determine physicians' fees.

The third major factor of RBRVS is the conversion factor (CF). The CF is a fixed-dollar amount that is multiplied by RVUs to establish the fee for a service provided. The CF is updated annually by CMS but is subject to change by legislation passed by Congress.

The fully implemented resource-based formula for calculating fees is:

$$[\ (RVUw \times GPCIw) + (RVUpe \times GPCIpe) + (RVUm \times GPCIm)\ ] \times CF$$

Another mandated consideration when calculating physicians' payment is budget neutrality (BN). In a growing program, BN accounts for program growth by reducing programmatic costs so that total program cost does not grow. A budget neutrality adjustment (BNA) that may change the formula when calculating physicians' fees may be applied in a given year.

In an attempt to properly represent the value of a procedure or service, CMS continually refines the Medicare Physician Fee Schedule (MPFS) based on research and credible input from groups such as the AMA's Relative Value Scale Update Committee (RUC). Annually CMS provides an updated MPFS to carriers. The MPFS that is published yearly can be downloaded from the CMS Website. Fortunately, medical office insurance staff members will not regularly be required to calculate fees but should be familiar with the process.

THE CORRECT CODING INITIATIVE

In addition to the role of the CPT code set, the ICD-9-CM code set, RVUs, GPCIs, and the CF in paying for physician services, the National Correct Coding Initiative (NCCI), or simply, the Correct Coding Initiative (CCI) — both acronyms are used interchangeably — was developed in 1996 to help control cost to the Medicare system. CMS recognized improper coding as a situation that was leading to improper payments to physicians. The greatest source of improper payments occurred when a combination of codes was reported. The intent of the CCI was to clarify how and when codes should be reported. Practically speaking, CCI gives instruction about which codes can be reported together and which must be reported separately. That is not to say that the CCI made physician billing easier for medical office insurance staff. Remember that the AMA is responsible for the CPT codebook. CMS relied on the CPT codebook to base its policies relating to the CCI and to define coding conventions to use as a payment guide for Medicare contractors.

To help sort out information, CMS supports a coding policy manual called the *National Correct Coding Initiative Coding Policy Manual for Medicare Services* that is updated annually. The manual may be acquired in two different ways. It may be downloaded from the CMS Website at www.cms.hhs.gov/NationalCorrectCodInitEd/. Alternately, the manual can be purchased in its entirety in printed and electronic form or in sections from the National Technical Information Service (NTIS). NTIS provides access for purchase from its Website including an electronic version at www.ntis.gov/products/families/cci/. It may also be purchased by calling 1-800-363-2068 toll free or 1-703-605-6060.

CCI breaks down edits into two sets of tables. Using these tables is not intuitive and, in fact, they can be difficult to understand. Exhibit 3.1 shows the two CCI edits tables in a side-by-side comparison. The first table is marked A, and the second table is marked B. The first table is defined as the *Column 1/ Column 2 Correct Coding Edits*, formerly called Comprehensive/Component. The *Column 1* portion, referred to in the title, represents what has been known as comprehensive code edits. The *Column 2* portion represents what has been known as component code edits. The second table contains *Mutually Exclusive Edits*.

Each table contains two columns: Column 1 and Column 2. However, the Column 1 codes and the Column 2 codes are defined differently in each of the two tables. Because Column 1 is defined differently in the first table than it is in the second table, these two tables are more difficult to understand and remember. Likewise, Column 2 is defined differently in the first table than it is in the second table.

To break down the two tables for understanding, look first at the *Column 1/ Column 2 Correct Coding Edits* table. This table includes two kinds of code pair edits, but the two kinds are not obvious. The first kind of code pair is the combination of Column1 comprehensive codes and Column 2 component codes.

The second, less obvious, kind of code is not related to the comprehensive/ component relationship. Rather, the second kind of code pair edits includes codes that simply should not be reported together. In other words, if these codes are reported together, it is a misuse of the code. This second kind of edit is the reason the name of the column was changed from Comprehensive/ Component to *Column 1/Column 2 Coding Edits*. Certain pairs of CPT codes and Healthcare Common Procedure Coding System (HCPCS) Level II codes should not be paid separately unless certain circumstances exist. The CCI edits address these code pairs when the same beneficiary receives more than one service

EXHIBIT 3.1 ■ CCI Edits Tables

	A	B
	Column 1/Column 2 Correct Coding Edits	**Mutually Exclusive Edits***
Column 1 means	Comprehensive code for a major procedure or service and represents a higher work RVU (RVUw) value	Procedure or service with a lower work RVU (RVUw) value
Column 2 means	Component code that is integral part of the Column 1 code and represents a lower work RVU (RVUw) value than the Column 1 code	Procedure or service with a higher work RVU (RVUw) value (When the higher work RVU code of Column 2 is reported with the Column 1 code, the Column 2 code is the procedure that will not be paid.)

*Mutually Exclusive Edits outline procedures or services that cannot reasonably be performed at the same session by the same provider on the same beneficiary. Both codes are paid only when indicated by clinical circumstances and billed with the appropriate modifier. Without the correct modifiers, only the Column 1 code will be paid. Modifiers must justify for Column 2 code to also be paid.

by the same provider on one date of service. Modifiers that should be used in these instances are also provided.

To reiterate, in the first table, Column 1 represents a comprehensive code. The Column 1 code is not only defined as the comprehensive code, but also the Column 1 code is generally the major procedure or service and represents a higher work RVU (RVUw) value than the code in Column 2. The Column 2 code differs from the Column 1 code in that it represents a lower work RVU value than the Column 1 code. In reality the definitions of Column 1 and Column 2 in the *Column 1/Column 2 Correct Coding Edits* table are simple but confusing. In short, Column 1 means comprehensive and major procedure with higher RVU, and Column 2 is a component code with a lesser RVU.

The second table is the *Mutually Exclusive Edits* table. This table includes edits pertaining to two codes that cannot be performed together either because of reasonableness, code definitions, or anatomic considerations. Again, this table consists of Column 1 and Column 2 codes, but the Column 1 codes and the Column 2 codes carry different definitions relating to this table. In the *Mutually Exclusive Edits* table, Column 1 indicates the procedure or service with the lower work RVU (RVUw). The Column 2 code indicates the procedure or service with the higher work RVU value. *The Mutually Exclusive Edits* table uses definitions of Column 1 and Column 2 that are exactly opposite definitions of those used for Column 1 and Column 2 in the *Column 1/Column 2 Correct Coding Edits* table.

The *Mutually Exclusive Edits* table addresses code pairs in which the same beneficiary receives more than one service by the same provider on one date of service. It also provides the modifiers that should be used in these instances if the code is to be paid. Without the appropriate modifier, only the Column 1 code will be paid. Only if clinical circumstances exist such that an appropriate and justifiable modifier is added to the Column 2 code will both the Column 1 and Column 2 codes be paid. When the higher work RVU code of Column 2 is reported with the Column 1 code, the Column 2 code is the procedure or service that will not be paid.

As noted, the *Mutually Exclusive Edits* table outlines procedures or services that cannot reasonably "be performed at the same session by the same provider on the same beneficiary" and contains edits that dictate when both codes will be paid — both codes are paid only if indicated by clinical circumstances and billed with the appropriate modifier. CCI edits allow three kinds of modifiers:

- Anatomical modifiers;
- Global surgery modifiers; and
- Other modifiers.

Allowed modifiers can be found at the CMS Website.

To recap the definitions of the two columns in the two tables: Column 1 represents the higher work RVU in the first table (*Column 1/Column 2 Correct Coding Edits*), but Column 1 represents the lower work RVU in the second table (*Mutually Exclusive Edits*). On the other hand, Column 2 represents the lower work RVU in the first table (*Column 1/Column 2 Correct Coding Edits*), but Column 2 represents the higher work RVU in the second table (*Mutually Exclusive Edits*).

In CCI, each code pair is assigned one of three modifier indicators: 0, 1, or 9. "0" indicates that a code pair cannot have any modifiers. "1" indicates that appropriate modifiers may be used. "9" refers to effective dates (which are of little consequence to medical office insurance staff).

To complicate the CCI further, CMS introduces Medically Unlikely Edits (MUEs) into the mix. In the Frequently Ask Questions (FAQ) section of the CMS Website, ID #8734, an MUE is defined as a "unit of service (UOS) edit for a Healthcare Common Procedure Coding System (HCPCS)/Current Procedural Terminology (CPT) code for services rendered by a single provider/supplier to a single beneficiary on the same date of service.[1] The ideal MUE is the maximum UOS that would be reported for a HCPCS/CPT code on the vast majority of appropriately reported claims. The MUE program provides a method to report medically reasonable and necessary UOS in excess of an MUE." These MUEs are identified based on data collected from correctly reported claims.

CMS states that the MUE program "provides a method to report medically reasonable and necessary UOS in excess of an MUE." However, CMS has not published MUEs because these "levels are confidential information that should not be published by third parties who have attempted to acquire them."

CMS is clear that modifiers used inappropriately (that is, when clinical circumstances do not justify their use) constitutes fraud. Thus, compliance with CCI is necessary. CMS rejects any notion that the CCI program is secretive. CMS upholds that CCI is not isolated from input by organizations such as the AMA and other medical societies. In fact, comments from such organizations are seriously considered before changes in CCI are implemented. CCI edits are updated quarterly and, as stated at the beginning of the CCI discussion, the CCI *Policy Manual* is updated annually in October. However, the manual is not necessarily valid for a whole year because of the quarterly updates. In some quarters, updates are substantial; in others, there are relatively few changes.

It is imperative that a physician practice is aware of the updates to the CCI edits. Although some software that contains the CCI edits exists, CMS only recognizes the CMS Website and NTIS as official sources of information. CMS suggests that if physicians' offices need to verify correctness in using modifiers, the office staff should contact the local carrier's provider relations department to explain any issue that is unclear and to request an answer to the question in writing. (*Note:* As discussed in Chapter 1, your local carrier is the agency that has contracted with CMS to administer the Medicare program in your area. Your local carrier, medical administrative contractor (MAC), applies coverage rules to determine appropriate payment of claims.)

When a physician's office disagrees with specific CCI edits, comments should be submitted in writing to:

> *National Correct Coding Initiative*
> *Correct Coding Solutions LLC*
> *P O Box 907*
> *Carmel, IN 46082-0907*

Medical office insurance staff members may also hear of Outpatient Code Editor (OCE) edits. OCE is a different editing system from the CCI edits and is used to process hospital outpatient services. While CCI edits are included in the OCE, CCI edits are only one version behind the current edits. OCE edits are arranged in numerical order and are accompanied by a description of each edit and a claim disposition for each edit. CCI edits, on the other hand, consist of pairs of codes arranged in two tables. Should it be necessary to request clarification on OCE edits, call the Division of Outpatient Care (DOC) at CMS at 410-786-0378.

PATIENT PAPERWORK

The elements of billing and payment that have been reviewed so far in this chapter are complex, and the learning curve relating to each of these elements is steep. Each of these billing elements has been either adopted by or initiated by CMS, and medical group practices are bound by these constraints to be paid properly. Most CMS initiatives are followed by insurance carriers and pervasively affect health care insurance policies. Therefore, medical office insurance staff members must be familiar with these initiatives. Unfortunately, even if the elements of billing and payment are well understood by medical office insurance staff members, there is still no guarantee that the service will be paid unless the medical organization is diligent about obtaining correct and appropriate paperwork from the patient.

Insurance Cards

The most important piece of patient paperwork is the insurance card. The medical office staff members, usually the front desk, must have access to the patient's insurance card and be able to interpret the information on the card correctly. Then it is necessary to accurately put that information into the medical practice's computer system so that an insurance claim can be filed. Only if the information is processed correctly does the possibility exist for the physician to be paid correctly by the insurance carrier. If the carrier pays properly, the patient should pay the remaining balance or coinsurance (the portion of the fee for which the patient is responsible). However, if the insurance information is not processed correctly, the insurance carrier will not issue correct payment to the physician and, in some cases, the patient may be held responsible for the services.

Patient Identification

Medical practices have an obligation to ensure that the persons they treat are, in fact, who they say they are. Assurance of patient identification can be gained by scanning an official identification card such as a driver's license and by taking a picture of the patient that is retained in the medical record. (Electronic medical records provide a perfect format for housing this important identification.) Verifying patient identity promotes patient safety as well as serves as a valuable reimbursement tool in trying to collect for services.

Signature on File

Medical practices are well served to have the patient sign a document that assigns benefits and creates a financial agreement between the patient and the practice upon presenting for treatment at the first office visit. These multipurpose agreements are often titled "Signature on File, Assignment of Benefits, and Financial Agreement." The rationale of this multipurpose form is to ask patients to sign one document that can be retained by the medical practice so that the medical practice can satisfy several objectives. For example, the medical practice must have the patient's cooperation in agreeing to allow the patient's insurance carrier to send payment directly to the physician and in agreeing to accept financial responsibility for services if insurance does not cover the service.

The initial purpose of this multipurpose form is to ensure that the medical practice is paid directly by the insurance carrier. The form also authorizes the medical practice to release information to the carrier so that a determination for payment of benefits can be made. The form may refer specifically to Item 9 of the CMS 1500 form for payment, which designates Medicare as the primary carrier and Medigap as the secondary insurance policy. Generally the form explains to the patient that the patient is financially responsible for payment of services rendered, and, if signed, constitutes an acknowledgment of financial responsibility on the part of the patient. This form must use language that causes the patient, by signing the form, to agree to be financially responsible for the co-payment, deductible, coinsurance, and services that are not covered by their benefit package. Language should be clear that if the medical practice does not have a contract with the patient's insurance carrier, the patient accepts full financial responsibility for charges and will sign over to the practice any payment from an insurance carrier that is made to the patient rather than to the practice.

Another important component of this multipurpose form is to obtain permission from the patient to release the patient's personal and medical information to other health care providers. This release-of-information component not only guarantees payment from the patient but also allows for the continuation of care for the patient.

The form may also address release of information for medical educational and scientific purposes relating to medical advancement and medical research. When an organization has a need to take medical photographs, the form should contain a section that grants permission of photographs. The medical practice should be specific in disclosing the purpose of the photograph and whether the patient will be identifiable from the photograph. Some release-of-information forms also contain sections called Informed Consent for Treatment. Neither the photograph section nor the Informed Consent section of the multipurpose form are particularly relevant to medical office insurance staff, but other aspects of the form are significant. The patient's signature on this form serves as a contract between the patient and the practice that is invaluable for the medical office insurance staff members to refer to when trying to resolve the patient's account.

INSURANCE VERIFICATION

Patients may have both primary and secondary insurance, and it can be difficult to determine which insurance is primary and which is secondary. Often patients do not know which of their insurance policies is primary and which is secondary. Medicare provides rules that determine when Medicare is a patient's primary or secondary insurance. It is the responsibility of the physician's office, specifically the medical office insurance staff members, acting on the physician's behalf, to determine whether Medicare is primary or secondary. For example, a Medicare patient may have Medicare as the primary insurance, but if a patient is seeking services for injuries resulting from an auto accident, Medicare will not be primary if auto insurance will cover the medical expenses. In this case the auto insurance is the primary insurance and Medicare is the secondary payer. In this and many other situations, knowledge of Medicare regulations is required to file the insurance claim correctly.

The patient's insurance card is often helpful in determining primary and secondary benefits, but unfortunately the card is not always foolproof in making the determination. Ideally, an insurance card should contain several pieces of information to assist in proper claim filing: the name of the insured, the name of the holder of the card seeking payment of health care services when that person is not the insured, and the relationship of the person seeking health care services to the insured. A card should also have a policy or group number clearly visible and an eligibility period for coverage benefits. Information relating to the insurance plan's co-payment amounts (the amount of required payment from the patient at the time of service) and deductible (the amount the insured patient must pay before insurance benefits begin) are also important. In addition, a toll-free phone number and the paying entity's address should be obvious on the card. No standardized format for insurance cards has been mandated in the United States, so there is wide disparity between insurance cards. Some insurance cards include all of the aforementioned information while others lack information.

Some cards are imprinted with the policyholder's name, or the insured name, or both. Other insurance cards are not imprinted at all. Rather, these are generic cards that have an individual's name hand-written or typed on the card. Medical office staff members in receipt of such cards may be unsure who is insured, whether the bearer of the card is the insured, or what the relationship of the cardholder may be to the insured. Insurance cards differ greatly from carrier to carrier, network to network, and third-party payer to third-party payer. Sometimes cards even differ from policy to policy when issued by a single carrier. A single carrier may use an unlimited number of card styles, each style bearing different information.

Whenever electronic verification of insurance is possible, medical practices should take advantage of that opportunity. Often front desk personnel claim that they do not have time to verify insurance. If this is the case, managers should support adding personnel to provide that function or should assign that task to existing personnel. The added effort to verify insurance coverage will pay off financially for the medical practice. At a minimum, the organization should disclose to the patient that insurance coverage has not been verified and that the patient will be responsible for payment if the insurance carrier does not cover the charges for the service. Disclosure will give the patient an opportunity to sign an "addition to form" for the Signature on File, Assignment of Benefits, and Financial Agreement indicating that he or she understands the situation.

An understanding of the Medicare rules for determining when Medicare is primary or secondary insurance is important for proper insurance verification. Although Medicare is the primary payer for many beneficiaries, it is not always the primary payer. Certainly, when there is no other insurance, Medicare is the primary payer. Medicare becomes the secondary payer when there are other possible payers. Other possible payers include:

- No fault or liability insurance;
- Workers' compensation;

- Employer group health plans if the individual or spouse is still working and covered by employer-sponsored insurance or other programs such as the Federal Employee Health Benefit Plan or military coverage provided by Veterans Affairs or TRICARE;
- The Federal Black Lung Program; or
- COBRA (Consolidated Omnibus Budget Reconciliation Act) continuation coverage.
- Medicare provides a coordination of benefits (COB) contractor who functions to identify benefits that may exist to the beneficiary that would put Medicare in a position to be the secondary payer. The COB contractor's role is to make sure that payments are coordinated so that no payment mistakes occur. The COB contractor will answer general questions regarding Medicare Secondary Payer (MSP), which is the term Medicare uses when Medicare is not the primary payer. Following are examples of when Medicare is the primary payer and when it is the secondary payer[2]:
  - If a patient has Medicare insurance but is covered by an employer-sponsored group health plan, and that employer has fewer than 20 employees, Medicare is the primary payer and the group health plan is the secondary payer.
  - If a patient has Medicare insurance but is covered by an employer-sponsored group health plan, and that employer has 20 or more employees, the group health plan is the primary payer and Medicare is the secondary payer.
  - If a patient has Medicare insurance and an employer-sponsored retirement plan, or if the patient is disabled, Medicare is the primary payer and the retiree coverage pays secondary.
  - If a patient is a disabled Medicare beneficiary and is covered by an employer-sponsored large group health plan of fewer than 100 employees, Medicare is the primary payer and the large group health plan is the secondary payer.
  - If a patient is a disabled Medicare beneficiary and is covered by an employer-sponsored large group health plan of 100 or more employees, the large group health plan is the primary payer and Medicare is the secondary payer.
  - If a patient has end stage renal disease (ESRD) and an employer-sponsored group health plan and is in the first 30 months of Medicare eligibility, the group health plan is the primary payer and Medicare is the secondary payer.
  - If a patient has ESRD and an employer-sponsored group health plan, and has been entitled to Medicare for 30 months or longer, Medicare is the primary payer and the group health plan is the secondary payer.
  - If a patient has ESRD and COBRA coverage and is in the first 30 months of Medicare eligibility, COBRA is the primary payer and Medicare is the secondary payer.
  - If a patient has ESRD and COBRA and has been entitled to Medicare for 30 months or longer, Medicare is the primary payer and COBRA is the secondary payer.

- If a patient is covered by workers' compensation insurance due to a job-related mishap and the patient is entitled to Medicare, workers' compensation is the primary payer and Medicare is the secondary payer.

- If a patient has been involved in a situation covered by no-fault or liability insurance and is entitled to Medicare, the no-fault or liability insurance is the primary payer and Medicare is the secondary payer.

The provider organizations have the responsibility of determining whether Medicare is the primary payer or if another form of insurance should pay before Medicare. This determination should be made at the front desk of the medical practice during registration; otherwise, the insurance claim may be filed to the wrong carrier. If Medicare pays as primary when another carrier should have been the primary payer, Medicare will recover the payment.

ROLE OF HIPAA

The most important aspect of HIPAA for medical office insurance staff members is the HIPAA Privacy Rule. The intent of the Privacy Rule is to protect an individual's personal and identifiable health information. HIPAA defines the use and disclosure of protected health information (PHI) and allows the individual as a patient to be secure in the knowledge that his or her personal health information will not be shared except as minimally necessary. (The entire HIPAA Privacy Rule can be found at www.hhs.gov/ocr/hipaa.) The Office for Civil Rights (OCR) within the U.S. Department of Health and Human Services has responsibility for enforcing the HIPAA Privacy Rule.

The standards required for electronic exchange of health information must be adhered to by all covered entities. A *covered entity* is any health care provider, person, or organization, regardless of size, that provides medical or health services, including health plans and health care clearinghouses. These entities are bound by HIPAA. In other words, any person or organization "that furnishes, bills, or is paid for health care" is subject to HIPAA regulations. All PHI that is held or transmitted by a covered entity in any form whether electronic, paper, or oral is protected by HIPAA. The Privacy Rule is intended to define the circumstances of disclosure and to limit the disclosure of an individual's health information. It is not intended to halt the flow of health information that is needed to provide high-quality health care.

The limits of disclosure are specific. A covered entity may disclose an individual's PHI when relating to treatment, payment, and other health care operations such as quality and improvement activities, medical reviews or audits, insurance functions, and public interest and benefit activities. Individuals have a right to their own PHI, and a covered entity must disclose information when requested by the patient or the patient's representatives. The Privacy Rule requires health care providers to:

- Make patients aware of their privacy rights;
- Implement privacy procedures within their organization;
- Name a privacy official to ensure adoption of privacy procedures; and
- Secure records with individually identifiable health information.

Although organizations must make patients aware of their privacy rights and make an effort to acquire acknowledgment that the patient received a notice of rights, it is not necessary to notify patients again if the facility changes its privacy policy. Organizations have the latitude to adopt privacy procedures that fit its needs.

Organizations must train employees relating to the Privacy Policy — training may be as simple as reviewing and documenting knowledge of the organization's privacy policy. The Privacy Rule permits an organization to charge a reasonable fee to cover the cost of copying and postage if medical records are requested. The organizations cannot charge staff labor costs for searching and retrieving information.

The Privacy Rule allows covered entities to cooperate with law enforcement officials without written authorization from the patient. In general, the Privacy Rule recognizes the importance of the legal process and is not at odds with answering court orders; reporting child or adult abuse, neglect, or domestic violence; and acting reasonably to prevent a health or public safety event. In each of these events the covered entity may rely on the law enforcement officials to define the minimum amount of information to suit the lawful purpose. It is the covered entities' responsibility to verify the identity and authority of law enforcement officials prior to disclosing information.

COMPLIANCE

Further affecting medical offices is the Office of Inspector General's Compliance Program for Individual and Small Group Physician Practices. In an attempt to encourage self-policing in the health care industry, the Office of Inspector General (OIG) issued in October 2000 a step-by-step approach for medical practices to use as guidelines to develop and implement voluntary compliance programs.[3] The compliance guidelines evolved from the Federal Sentencing Guidelines. While the OIG compliance guidelines do not have the same legal significance as the Federal Sentencing Guidelines, they are significant. Most health care matters do not go before federal judges; rather enforcement agencies such as the OIG initiate health care investigations. "Having a corporate compliance program which OIG considers effective can influence the enforcement environment in many ways, including:

- Who gets investigated and how;
- Whether investigation is civil or criminal;
- What matters are prosecuted, and by whom;
- Whether and on what terms the government will settle;
- Whether the government will impose its own compliance program through a corporate integrity agreement, and how stringent that will be; and
- Who gets excluded from Medicare and Medicaid."[4]

The OIG compliance guidelines are focused on reimbursement and regulatory issues of federal health care. As noted in the title of the guidance, the guidelines apply to small groups. However, the OIG does not define a small group. It is generally considered that these guidelines apply to any physician medical practice that does not have a full-time compliance department.[3]

The OIG is particularly interested in fraudulent claims. It hopes to reduce erroneous claims in the areas of coding and billing, medical necessity, documentation, kickbacks, and self-referral. The OIG guidance outlines the following seven-step approach[5]:

- Internal monitoring and auditing;
- Written standards and procedures;
- A designated compliance officer;
- Education and training;
- Investigations and disclosure;
- Lines of communication that are open; and
- Disciplinary standards that are enforced.

The cornerstone of the compliance guidance is the Documentation Guidelines for Evaluation and Management (E/M) Services. Physician practices may use either the 1995 or the 1997 E/M guidelines to begin the first step of the seven-step compliance approach. Internal monitoring and auditing is predicated on compliance with the E/M guidelines. Each of the other six steps in compliance, as outlined earlier, follows based on the degree of conformity with the E/M guidelines. The presence of a formalized compliance plan in a health care organization signals that a physician organization intends to conduct all of its affairs by the rules and regulations governing federal health policy.

CLAIMS FORMAT

Health care providers and the billing services and clearinghouses representing them have specific mandated rules that affect the electronic transmission of data. Those requirements are a provision of HIPAA and are responsible for CMS adopting national standards ($\times$12 837) for Electronic Data Interchange (EDI) transactions and further for the paper claims that correspond with those electronic claims. These rules apply to claims that are submitted to or from Medicare. The information governing claims transfer and outlining the requirements relating to the COB can be found in the *Medicare Claims Processing Manual*. (*Note:* In 2003 CMS transformed the paper-based, hard-copy manuals to the CMS Online Manual System called Internet-only manuals [IOMs]. While most of the paper-based manuals were transferred to the IOM, paper-based manuals still exist for reference purposes. If you find policy information contained in the hard-copy manuals that are not included in IOMs, a message can be sent to CMS via the Feedback tool. For practical purposes of storage and current information, medical office insurance staff should consult the IOM from the CMS Website. The online manuals can be accessed at www.cms.hhs.gov/Manuals/IOM/list.asp.

The HIPAA regulation has provided a uniform standard for transactions, which are defined as any activity that transfers health information between one entity to another for a specific purpose, as well as for code sets and identifiers. These are called Transaction and Code Sets Standards. The transactions standard affects claims information, claims payment, claims remittance advice, claims status, and claims inquiry. Although the language is different, medical office insurance staff members are already familiar with code sets. Examples of code sets are CPT codes, ICD-9 codes, and HCPCS codes. These code sets identify E/M services, procedures, and diagnoses. (A series of 10 papers that discusses the Transaction and Code Sets Standards in depth can be found on the CMS Website at www.cms.hhs.gov/EducationMaterial/02_HIPAAMaterials.asp#TopOfPage or www.cms.hhs.gov from home page. From this page search "Transaction and Code Sets Standards." This will take you to the Transaction and Code Sets Standards Overview, where you can click on related link HIPAA Information Series for Providers.)

The EDI system is an important issue for medical office insurance staff members. They must be aware that each new provider is required to participate in EDI enrollment in order to exchange transaction information. The agreement, called the CMS Standard EDI Enrollment Form, confirms the provider's responsibility to safeguard all data relating to PHI. In addition, the agreement specifies who is authorized to exchange data on behalf of the provider and instructs that the provider must notify the Medicare contractor if that information should change.

This national standard also supports Electronic Funds Transfer (EFT) so that funds can be deposited directly into the provider's account in a financial institution. The EFT authorization form, as a part of Medicare enrollment, should be completed and sent with a voided blank check indicating the facility and account in which funds from Medicare will be transferred. EFT facilitates a faster transfer of funds to providers whether claims are filed electronically or on paper. It takes Medicare funds approximately two weeks to be transferred into the account directed by the provider.

The elements of health care insurance billing and payment discussed in this chapter are largely initiated and directed by CMS for Medicare beneficiaries. To reiterate, commercial carriers follow the lead of Medicare. Due to regulatory requirements, it is important for every medical office insurance staff member to be well acquainted with Medicare regulations.

References

1. Access www.cms.hhs.gov/defalt.asp? Then click on Resources & Tools. Under Sitewide Tools & Resources; click on Frequently Asked Questions; enter search term MUE. The quote is from #8734.

2. *Medicare Secondary Payer Fact Sheet.* Available at www.cms.hhs.gov/mlnproducts/downloads/msp_fact_sheet.pdf.

3. *Federal Register*, October 5, 2000, p. 59434.

4. Brandt, K., and Saner, R. J. (Speakers). 2000. *Final Rule—OIG Small Group Compliance* (Audio Conference, November 7, 2000). Denver: Medical Group Management Association.

5. *Federal Register*, October 5, 2000, p. 59434.

CHAPTER FOUR

Importance of Insurance in the Revenue Cycle

Management of the revenue cycle in medical practices has evolved into one of the practice's most important and complex operational tasks. Good revenue cycle management can ensure an organization's financial viability, whereas poor management can result in the demise of a medical practice's independence. In a viable medical practice, both managers and staff members must understand the elements of the revenue cycle and continually work toward improving "getting the money in the door."

ELEMENTS OF THE REVENUE CYCLE

Medical office insurance staff members play a critical role in the revenue cycle in physicians' organizations. Yet rarely are they exposed to the entire breadth of the revenue cycle and often lack information about where their role fits into the whole process. They focus intently on the work they do, unaware of its larger context. The quality of their work can be improved by a better understanding of its place in the organization's revenue cycle.

Contracting

The revenue cycle begins when physicians' organizations contract with health care insurance carriers. All contracts are not equal. Each contract is payer specific and sets out the terms of the agreement between the payer and the provider. Some payers allow some providers to negotiate fees, while other payers do not. Some providers are required to adhere strictly to the published fee schedule.

Much of the success of contract negotiating depends on the ability of the person doing the contract negotiating for the provider. Contract negotiating is both an art and a science. The science involved is in knowing the details of the practice in terms of tangible information such as patient population spread, which procedures and services are frequently provided, and which ones are rarely provided. For example, if the particular contract negotiated will affect one third of the patients in the practice, then fees become very important. This is especially true for the high-volume procedures or services. On the other hand, if the contract affects less than one percent of the patient population, fees for the high-volume procedures and services are not as important. In fact, there may be no need to devote the time and energy to participate with a payer in this category.

Tangible information about the practice can also be used to give the insurance carrier patients' impressions relating to satisfaction and quality. Certainly, this kind of information affects how much a payer wants a physician organization to become a participating organization. If this kind of information cannot be produced, then the art of contract negotiation comes into play. The individual negotiating for the practice must help create perception. It is worthwhile for the payer's representative to understand the importance of adding this practice to its panel of providers and how that addition will benefit the payer.

In addition to fees, contracts dictate all other terms, such as renewal and termination parameters, timely filing limits, methods of contacting the payer, claims adjudication, and information regarding notifications from the payer regarding changes in the contract. These terms of the contract are of particular significance to medical office insurance staff. Although it is not typical for medical office insurance staff members to participate in contract negotiations, they can be instrumental in making sure that payers reimburse as they have agreed to reimburse for services provided. Good insurance staff shows vigilance in paying attention and noting when payers suddenly begin paying a different amount on a service. These changes should be appealed no matter how small. Otherwise the payer will continue to short the practice. Over time even a small difference in reimbursement can become a significant amount of lost revenue.

A contracted rate with a payer should cover both the physician's services and the overhead required to provide the services. Poorly negotiated contracts put the medical practice at a disadvantage because contract terms can affect the practice for years to come. Some carriers try to find as many reasons as possible to withhold or reduce payment. If contracted rates don't cover both the overhead of providing the service and the process of collecting for that service, the rates are too low to sustain the practice.

Information Collection

Information collection is typically the responsibility of front desk personnel. However, the correctness of the information collected greatly affects the work of medical office insurance staff members. The information gathered from a new patient to the practice should include all of the obvious identifying demographic information such as the patient's name, date of birth, and contact information. The information should also include the patient's phone numbers, email address, referring physician, primary care physician (if applicable), emergency contact, authorization for release of information as well as names of persons to whom information can be released, assignment of benefits, insurance coverage waiver if insurance isn't confirmed, and insurance information.

Scanning and retaining patients' identification cards by electronic storage enables the entire medical practice access to important patient information. Scanning cards is a process that can be implemented fairly inexpensively and with little hold up at the front desk. Cards that should be scanned include insurance cards, both primary and secondary, and the patient's driver's license.

The insurance card should be scanned at every visit — employers change insurance coverage sometimes without patients realizing the implication of the change to their benefits structure, particularly if they stay with the same carrier or remain in the same network. Without question, patients who are not accustomed to bringing their insurance cards to the physician's office at every visit may think this policy doesn't make any sense. For the patients who resist this policy, an analogy can be used to help them understand: If you eat at a restaurant three days consecutively and charge your meal on your credit card each day, you must produce the card each day to pay. Once patients get the concept that their insurance card is their health care credit card, most will comply. Access to correct information every time the patient comes into the practice can ensure that claims are sent to the right carrier. Claims that go to the correct carrier are reimbursed more quickly, and cash is turned faster.

Equally important to gathering the correct information is entering the information correctly into the organization's computer system. Data entry mistakes made by front desk personnel are a common cause of frustration for medical office insurance staff members. A group number that is entered incorrectly can delay payment of a claim for weeks until the mistake is discovered. Practices should create a process that minimizes front desk errors.

Charge Capture

Charge capture refers to the process of assigning the appropriate charges for every billable procedure or service delivered to the patient by a provider so that money can be collected for them. Charge capture is often a joint effort in the practice. Clearly, providers who provide service have the primary responsibility to initiate and capture charges.

Medical practices vary in their sophistication relating to the ability to integrate electronic medical records with electronic charge capture capabilities. A great many organizations still wait for the physicians to dictate charges, which must then be transcribed, coded, and finally posted as a charge to a patient's account. Organizations that intend to sufficiently capture charges for a date of service in a short time frame should create an organizational standard about the amount of time that is permitted to lapse between a service provided and the charge entered into the practice management system to be billed. Unless the issue of timely and accurate charge capture is addressed and agreed upon at the physician level, the process will likely come up short of ideal.

Medical office insurance staff members lack the authority to put charge capture policies in place, but they can make their supervisors and administrators aware when timeliness is an issue. Administrators can then point out to physicians what a detriment poor charge capture habits are to the entire practice.

Sometimes fellow physicians are the best at pointing out to another physician the problems with poor charge capture. Medical office insurance staff members should empower themselves to advocate for effective charge capture processes and policies, and to notify their practice managers if those processes are not followed. Better efficiencies throughout the medical practice make the work of getting the money in the door easier to accomplish.

Charge Entry

Accuracy and timeliness are of utmost importance in charge entry. Once the charge is captured, logically, charge entry follows. This straightforward step can often be less efficient than it should be. First, a process for accurate charge entry must be established and followed. Charges posted in the computer system should balance to the charge tickets of every batch posted every day. Charge entry affects the practice both from a financial and patient satisfaction standpoint. It is not enough to get the charge posted; it must be posted to the correct account and posted accurately.

Charges must also be posted promptly. Patients know when services are provided, and they expect members of the medical practice to know as well. When they have an interaction with the practice whose representative is not aware of services that have been provided, the patient may lose confidence in the practice. Patients are more apt to accept the responsibility to pay charges when they feel assured that the practice is on top of both providing the services and charging for the services. An organization that is financially tight inspires confidence in patients.

Regardless of the charge entry process, it is imperative for the medical practice to ensure that charge entry and charge capture processes have been given adequate planning attention. Likewise, monitoring must take place to ensure that the processes are being carried out. These two important functions in the medical practice cannot be treated as haphazard afterthoughts.

Generating and Submitting Claims

Electronic claims should be filed every day to ensure a short time frame between the date of providing service and submitting the claim for payment. The quicker a claim is filed after the date of service, the sooner that claim will be paid. In addition, timely filing increases the likelihood that the claim will be paid as billed. Most organizations that file claims quickly know this anecdotally. Their aging analysis provides evidence that quick turnaround pays off.

Electronic claims formatting is particularly at risk when organizations move to a new informational technology system. It is the organization's contracted computer vendor/information technology (IT) partner that does electronic claims formatting. Yet it is essential that the person working in the medical practice who is communicating with the information technology company on claims formatting understand the billing needs of the organization. The medical practice's liaison must be able to communicate those needs to the IT representative and stand firm in his or her requests. Likewise, it is necessary that the IT representatives listen to the organization's personnel and accurately program what the organization needs.

The financial ramifications of incorrect electronic claims formatting cannot be overstated. If the right combinations of billing group number, procedure, place of service, physician, and modifiers are not set correctly, payment will not be made correctly. These mistakes have a compounding effect on the insurance department. Now medical office insurance staff not only have the volume of claims to keep up with but also receive an influx of incorrect claims due to mistakes made in getting the claim out the door.

Good records relating to the setup of electronic claims formatting are indispensable to medical organizations. Without question there will be staffing changes in the practice. Just as certain, there will be need for changes to the electronic claims format. Without good documentation of the initial setup of electronic claims formatting, the organization is at risk for making changes that are broader than necessary for the issue at hand. Unintended consequences can occur even with a small change if the change is not well thought through. Mistakes of this kind can take weeks to identify and can put the organization at financial risk. It is incumbent on organizational management to take electronic claims formatting seriously and assign the proper level of supervision to the process.

Working Claims

Once a claim pays the patient or provider, the organization receives information from the carrier about the amount of payment remitted for medical services. A form, known as an explanation of benefits (EOB), accompanies each remittance for an insurance claim. The staff members must interpret the EOB precisely so that payment can be accurately applied against the charge for services rendered. Payments applied incorrectly affect the balance the patient owes on the service. In addition, medical office insurance staff members may discover from information indicated on the EOB that services have not been paid correctly. In this event, an appeal must be filed with the insurance carrier. If an appeal is not filed, the physician's reimbursement for the services rendered will be incorrect — usually shorted. In fact, both the patient's service balance and the physician's reimbursement may be altered by inaccurately interpreting the EOB.

Interpreting the EOB is complicated by the lack of standardization of insurance cards and EOBs. The complexity of the process is increased by the variety of organizations that pay health care insurance benefits. Only a few of the payment methods can be touched on here to illustrate the problem.

First, the most direct method of payment is for the insurance company/carrier to provide payment directly to the physician or the patient. If payment is made directly to the physician, medical office insurance staff members acting on the physician's behalf are responsible to bill the patient for the balance of the service. If the patient is paid directly, the patient is responsible to pay the physician both the portion paid by the insurance carrier and the remainder of the balance.

Second, the insurance company may be part of a network with a special pricing agreement with the physician. In this case claims are filed through the network for re-pricing before they are sent to the insurance carrier for payment. Payment is made directly to the physician, with the patient paying the physician according to the design of the patient's insurance plan.

Third, an insurance company may use a third-party payer to adjudicate claims before the carrier makes payment. In this case the check may be sent out for an individual's services from the third-party payer while the third-party payer in turn collects from the insurance company. Opportunity for error exists because the insurance card may bear the name of the carrier, the network, the third-party payer, or all three.

Similarly, incongruity exists in EOB formats. EOBs may be difficult to read. They may not contain the specific information needed to apply the payment, and they may reflect incorrect benefit pricing. A medical facility must be able to tie the reimbursement from an EOB to the proper charges for credit application. This matching is done by the patient's name, date of birth, and/or social security number. The information on an EOB differs from the information on an insurance card in that the EOB must refer to the date of service, place of service, services provided for payment application, and attending physician. Like insurance cards, the information contained on EOBs and the formats of EOBs vary from carrier to carrier. Because the information is convoluted, the medical staff members processing payment from an insurance carrier are faced with pervasive ambiguity.

EXPLANATION OF BENEFITS

An EOB is sent from insurance companies to both providers and subscribers/patients when a claim is filed. The EOB informs the recipients about claims payment or action taken relating to a filed claim. Medical office insurance staff members rely heavily on EOBs to do their work. However, EOBs can add to the workload because subscribers/patients who are confused by the EOB often call the practice. Sometimes they think that the EOB is a bill and are unsure about what to do with it. The practice's insurance department staff members can be instructive in helping the patients/subscribers understand why they have received the EOB.

Reading EOBs

As noted earlier in this chapter, the EOB is not a consistent document, but they typically contain the same basic information. When reading the EOB, the medical office insurance staff members should first and foremost make sure that they are dealing with the right patient — for example, the patient's name, contract number, and group number should be verified. In a medical practice an EOB may be pages long, and the information on an EOB may affect many people. Once certainty of the correct patient is established, the EOB will contain such information as the date of service, a description of service, the place of service, the amount charged, the amount allowed, the impact of other insurance, the amount paid by the carrier, and reason code(s) for making the payment. Usually the EOB also includes a section relating to the patient's responsibility for payment based on the patient's purchased benefits contract. The EOB will show items such as co-payment amount, deductible, coinsurance, and amounts not covered.

Interpreting EOBs

Medical office insurance staff members are charged with the task of wading through the information on the EOB to make sure that the information is accurate and that the claim was paid correctly. Codes called "reason codes" are vital to understanding how the claim was paid. But the medical office insurance staff person may find that the reason code listed on the EOB is inappropriate for the situation. The lack of consistency of the EOB form plays to the advantage of the insurance carrier and is detrimental to the medical practice. If medical office insurance staff members simply post the payment as paid without scrutinizing whether the claim was paid correctly, practices stand to lose revenue.

EOBs contain critical information for payment posting. Unfortunately, when payment posting is complete, EOBs cannot be forgotten. In fact, EOBs contain information that needs to be accessed easily throughout account resolution and beyond. EOBs provide data for the insurance staff when patients or insurance carriers make inquiry. Even when the medical practice is satisfied that the account has been financially resolved, in the future the insurance carrier may raise issues with payment for services that were provided. Organizations should have a mechanism for scanning, indexing, and saving EOBs in the computer system for future use. Older EOBs should be saved to disk, like encounter tickets, so that they can be accessed to verify historical information.

Participation

If the organization has a contract with an insurance carrier, the difference between the amount charged and the allowed amount on the EOB will be the difference between the standard fee as the charged amount and the contracted fee as the allowed amount. At this juncture mistakes are often made both on the part of the payer and on the part of the insurance staff. For example, if a carrier suddenly starts paying the allowed amount at a lower rate than the contracted rate, it is the responsibility of insurance staff to note that difference and act to appeal the lower payment.

Organizations set up processes to work appeals differently based on factors within the organization; however, it is important to make sure that there is a process to identify claims that need to be appealed and follow-up procedures to ensure that those appeals are made to the carrier. It is also important for medical office insurance staff to understand that paying at a rate that is lower than the contracted amount may cost the medical practice significantly, even if it is a small amount of money. The cost can be particularly significant if the procedure or service is one that is a high-volume procedure or service.

A change in a payment amount may occur because the fee has been reset by the carrier. Even if the change is not a deliberate act of malice toward the organization, the carrier must be called on the change. If the organization has negotiated a fee that is different than the carrier's standard fees for providers in that specialty, the carrier is obligated to pay the negotiated rate unless otherwise stated in the contract. If the inappropriate payment is not noted to the carrier as incorrect, the fee will stand and will continue to be paid at the lower rate.

Non-Participation

A provider who does not participate with an insurance carrier is not obligated to accept what the carrier pays as payment in full for services. Assume that the billed charge is $100, and the carrier allows $20 on that charge. The medical organization can then hold the patient responsible for the $80 balance.

Organizations must make decisions about how they communicate with patients when the organization does not participate with the carrier. Certainly, patients should have that information in advance of receiving services from the provider. They should know that the provider does not participate with the patient's insurance carrier. This information should be provided at the time of the patient's initial appointment. If communication is not made at that juncture, the information should be given at the time of new patient paperwork or check-in so that the patient can decide if he or she wants services from that provider. The patient receiving services should know that if he or she receives services offered by a provider who does not participate with his or her insurance carrier, the provider will not ensure that they receive a discount on billed charges. Optimally the issue will have already been discussed so that there are no holes in the provider's schedule.

PHYSICIAN CREDENTIALING

Before a physician can participate with an insurance carrier, the physician must be credentialed with the carrier. This is a time-consuming process, often taking up to six months to complete. Physicians and management must understand that this lengthy process requires the submission of extensive information that must be supplied by the physician who is being credentialed to the organization doing the credentialing. If enough time is not allowed, the physician will not be a participating provider when the physician begins work. The non-participation status may affect the relation between patients and the physician going forward if the situation is not handled carefully by the organization. This kind of situation must be dealt with within the organization. The best plan is to ensure that the physician is credentialed with the organization's health plans before the physician's effective employment date.

The medical organization should have a standard list of items that a newly hired physician must provide to the practice so that credentialing can take place. See Exhibit 4.1 for a sample physician credentialing checklist. Often physicians do not understand the significant amount of information required or the steps in the process. It is important that the organization help the

EXHIBIT 4.1 ■ Physician Credentialing Checklist

Items	Date Requested	Date Received	Date Sent	Sent To
1. Name				
2. CAQH Password				
3. Current State Licenses-Copy				
4. DEA-Copy (with address of new location)				
5. BNDD-Copy (with address of new location)				
6. CV-Current				
7. Date of Birth				
8. Social Security Number				
9. Practice Address: Location 1				
10. Practice Address: Location 2				
11. Practice Tax ID Number				
12. Practice Phone Number				
13. Practice Fax Number				
14. Practice Contact Each Location				
15. Physician NPI Number				
16. All Education (month and year of attendance, address for each institution, name of program director)				
17. All Training (month and year of attendance, address for each institution, name of program director)				
18. Hospital Affiliations (past, present, and pending)				
19. Practice Specialty (board certification/affiliation)				
20. Work History (10 years since completion of training)				
21. Professional Certificates (license numbers: include all state license current and past)				
22. Professional Liability Insurance (past 10 years: agent, address, policy number, and group name)				
23. Professional Liability Insurance (copy of current insurance with name, amount of coverage, expiration date/if name not on certificate, attach list of physicians covered by policy)				
24. Malpractice Claims History				
25. Hospital Privileges (sheet including education needed, proctoring requirements, and recent education completed)				
26. CME Documents				
27. Peer References (same degree and specialty notes with fax number)				
NOTES				

physician understand that the employment start date with the organization may be altered if the information is not submitted to the practice in a timely manner.

Of the many items on the standard list of items needed, a valid state medical license issued by the state in which the provider will be providing services is required. Acquiring a state license itself may take weeks to months. The medical organization should print a specific state license application to give to the new provider so that the practice will have complete and correct information, particularly if the practice is applying for state licensure for the provider. Items required for a state license application may include:

- Social security number;
- Date of birth;
- Name (exactly as it is to appear on license);
- Mailing address;
- Daytime phone number;
- Email address;
- Name as it appears on the physician's degree or other credentialing;
- Citizenship information;
- Personal conduct information such as:
  - Found or pleaded guilty or no contest to any felony or misdemeanor or pending court charges;
  - Any disciplinary action by a medical licensing authority;
  - Professional misconduct; and
  - Restricted privileges information.
- School information (beginning with high school to include postsecondary education, medical education, and a chronology of all experience or activities since beginning medical school), including:
  - Name of schools attended;
  - Locations;
  - Years attended;
  - Entrance and leaving dates; and
  - Title of diploma or degree (if conferred); if not conferred, credits earned.
- Information about where the physician will practice;
- Gender and ethnicity;
- Financial obligations, including loans and child support;
- Permission for the licensing authority to research education;
- Recent photograph; and
- Signed and notarized affidavit of truthfulness of the information provided.

Other necessary items for credentialing include current certificates from the Bureau of Narcotics and Dangerous Drugs (BNDD) and the U.S. Department of

Justice's Drug Enforcement Administration (DEA). A certificate from the BNDD is issued by the state. States are required to maintain a registry of persons who are authorized to prescribe and dispense controlled substances. Applications for BNDD can be found for each specific state on the state's department of health Website.

A certificate from the DEA is issued by the federal government. The DEA certificate cannot be issued until the applicant has shown proof that he or she has completed all of the state requirements for conducting business and received licensure in the state in which he or she intends to provide care. A DEA certificate will not be issued if the applicant cannot obtain state licensure. Likewise, if state licensure is revoked, DEA certification must be relinquished, and the state authority will also be revoked. Drugs are listed in schedules of controlled substances, and each application must be clear about which schedules of controlled substances the provider is asking to be authorized to prescribe or dispense. Every three years providers must renew the DEA registration. If a provider has more than one principal business location from which they will be dispensing controlled substances, an additional registration is required for each location. In addition, when a provider changes business addresses, the DEA certificate must be updated to reflect the new address. Address change request forms, as well as complete DEA information, may be found at www. DEAdiversion.usdoj.gov.

A physician's *curriculum vitae* is also a necessary part of licensure and credentialing. The curriculum vitae should contain the general identifying information relating to an applicant and the complete education and training history of the applicant. The education and training history should not only include addresses but also contact names within institutions such as the name of the program director. It is important that the information contained on each submitted document can be verified by the information on other documents. If not, each step in completing the credentialing process may be held up.

Work history should include all of the applicant's affiliations with hospitals where he or she has held privileges — including privileges that are pending as well as past and present privileges. In addition to hospital affiliations, the applicant must provide all professional associations, with months and years noted, since the completion of training or at least for the past 10 years. Any chronological gap must be explained. All current and past state licenses, professional certificates, and practice specialty information such as board certification should also be accessible.

An applicant's malpractice claims history is also necessary for the credentialing process. Claims history may be sent as an attachment with each claim's history outlined in detail. Even if an applicant doesn't have any claims, the claims report must be completed by noting as such.

An applicant's current medical liability insurance information such as coverage dates and limits must also be submitted. A certificate showing that the provider will have medical liability insurance with the group with whom he or she will be working may be required. Certainly, information relating to the practice that is credentialing the provider will be required such as practice address, tax identification number, phone and fax numbers, as well as a contact name and phone number in the practice where information can be clarified when questions arise. The provider's continuing medical education (CME) documentation may also be required.

The credentialing and re-credentialing process is an important issue in the insurance department of medical practices. In the past, the credentialing process has been so time-consuming for insurance departments that some states have agreed to mandate and accept a standardized credentialing form rather than allow each insurance carrier to dictate the format of the information used to do credentialing in its individual organization.

In addition, there are many third-party organizations that offer to do credentialing services online for providers to help relieve the credentialing burden. Some organizations offering services are for-profit organizations, while the Council for Affordable Quality Healthcare (CAQH) — a nonprofit alliance founded by many of the nation's large health plans and trade associations — offers a simplified approach to credentialing through its Universal Provider Datasource. CAQH is free to providers in all 50 states and in the District of Columbia and is an accepted format for credentialing with hundreds of health plans. CAQH uses a standard online form on which information can be revised and authorized for release to health plans as designated by providers. After becoming authorized to access information from the CAQH secure database, payers can then download the credentialing information to credential and re-credential providers. (The CAQH Website is www.caqh.org.) Even with the improvements made by using CAQH, credentialing is an additional chore that must be attended to on a regular basis.

DOCUMENTATION AND CODING

The Centers for Medicare & Medicaid Services (CMS) mandates specific requirements for the documentation and coding of medical services provided. Requirements were first laid out in 1995 and were followed by an additional set of requirements in 1997. The latest guidelines lay out the general principles of documentation for medical records.[1] Those principles rest on the belief that good documentation is critical to providing quality patient care. The patient record must give a chronological account of the patient's care in terms of pertinent facts relating to past and present illnesses along with findings and observations about the patient's health based on examinations, any tests ordered, treatment, and outcomes. The complete record aids in evaluating and managing the patient's health issues in the present and over time.

The medical office insurance staff members, while not responsible for the content of documentation, can be adept at understanding when documentation for an encounter does not support the charge level that was billed. When medical office insurance staff members understand documentation guidelines, they can better help the practice avoid compliance issues with billing. Payers require accurate information from documentation relating to date of service, site of service, medical necessity, and appropriateness of the service related to the diagnosis. Documentation must support the Current Procedural Terminology (CPT®)* and International Classification of Diseases, Ninth Revision (ICD-9) codes billed to the payers. The medical record must be legible even if hand written. Obviously, a typed, dictated, and transcribed, or computer-generated record is preferable.

Principles of the accurate patient record hold that the record should include the reason for the visit, an assessment of health risks including patient history, a physical exam pertinent to the presenting problem, rationale for any tests ordered or procedures done, clinical impression and diagnosis, as well as the patient's progress with treatment and changes in treatment. The three key components of the patient's medical record that document a provider's encounter with a patient are history, examination, and medical decision making. Each is discussed next.

E/M History

When documenting a patient's history, four elements should be included:

- **The Chief Complaint (CC).** The CC describes why the patient is seeing the provider at that encounter on that day. The CC can be stated in the patient's own words and should describe the problem and its signs or symptoms.

- **The History of Present Illness (HPI).** The HPI gives a chronological description, starting with the first sign or symptom (or last encounter) to the present. The elements that may be included in the HPI description are location, quality, severity, duration, timing, context, and modifying factors related to the main symptom, as well as associated signs and symptoms. Documentation relating to HPI may be brief or extended. If the HPI is brief, three of the elements from the list provided by Medicare should be included. If the HPI is extended, at least four elements from the list should be included.

- **Review of Systems (ROS).** ROS relates directly to the body areas and organ systems involved in the CC and takes an inventory of the organ system(s) related to the problem. Providers will use the ROS that best relates to the specialty medical services they provide.

- **The Past, Family, and/or Social History (PFSH).** The PFSH reviews three areas. First, the patient's past illnesses, injuries, treatments, and operations are reviewed. Second, the patient's family history is reviewed to look for hereditary or significant medical events that may influence the patient's risk. Third, to obtain a social history, the provider asks age-appropriate questions that may be related to the patient's problem.

The history section of the Documentation Guidelines is based on four billing levels that affect the extent of the HPI, ROS, and PFSH. These billing levels are: (1) Problem Focused, (2) Expanded Problem Focused, (3) Detailed, and (4) Comprehensive.

E/M Examination

There are two types of examinations: general multi-system examinations and single organ system examinations. The four levels of billing listed in the previous section apply to each of these examination types. A Problem-Focused examination, the lowest level of documentation, must evidence that one to five of the possible bulleted elements listed in elements of examination were examined in one or more organ systems or body areas.[1] Expanded Problem Focused, the second level of exam, must evidence that at least six bulleted elements were examined in one or more organ systems or body areas. Detailed, the third level of exam, progresses to the examination of at least six organ systems or body areas and the documentation of at least two bulleted elements in each system or 12 bulleted elements in two or more organ systems or body areas. Comprehensive, the highest level of exam, progresses to the examination of at least nine organ systems or body areas and the documentation of at least two bulleted elements in each system.

This provides a general overview of exam levels. A more detailed version of the Documentation Guidelines, necessary for medical record auditing, can be found on the CMS Website.

Medical Decision Making

Medical decision making refers to the amount of complexity involved in establishing a diagnosis and selecting management options for the patient. There are four types of medical decision making, ranging from straightforward decision making to making decisions of high complexity. These types are referred to as:

- Straightforward;
- Low complexity;
- Moderate complexity; and
- High complexity.

The elements of medical decision making to be considered include the number of management options based on the number of diagnoses to be considered during the encounter; the data to be reviewed based on the amount of data and its complexity such as tests ordered or planned; and the related risks of significant complications, morbidity, and/or mortality that are associated with the presenting problem.

Although medical office insurance staff members will not be accountable for medical decision making, they must be familiar with the types of medical decision making and the elements to be considered in each. For example, informed insurance staff members will know that if decision making for the presenting problem is straightforward and the level of risk is minimal, it is unlikely that a comprehensive examination is warranted or will pass a carrier's audit.

FRAUD AND ABUSE

The importance of the documentation process in medical practices cannot be overstated. The volume of claims filed and the billions of dollars represented by those claims make the insurance claims process susceptible to mistakes, fraud, and abuse. It should be understood that most errors made in health care billing are not attempts at fraud. Most errors are made because of a lack of knowledge on the part of parties such as providers, administration, and medical office insurance staff. Mistakes can be costly to honest providers, and it is incumbent on medical office insurance departments to make every effort to ensure that pursuing accuracy is an abiding rule in the medical practice. On the other hand, fraud and abuse occupy a different space in the medical organization and, for the benefit of all parties, must not be engaged in or tolerated. Understanding the differences in and definitions of fraud and abuse is important.

Fraud

Conversations on the topic of fraud in health care over the past decade have caused concern for many providers. Medicare has pursued and prosecuted providers who have not adhered to the guidelines of the Medicare program. Medicare has also used its resources to help states police providers against dishonest practices in order to retain billions of dollars that could be vulnerable to fraudulent practices. *Fraud* is defined in Title 18, of the U.S. code, as "knowingly and willingly executing, or attempting to execute, a scheme or artifice to defraud any health care benefit program or to obtain (by means of false or fraudulent pretenses, representations, or promises) any of the money or property owned by, or under the custody or control of, any health care benefit program."

The Medicare Integrity Program (MIP) was established under the Health Insurance Portability and Accountability Act (HIPAA) to achieve accuracy in health care reimbursement. Its goal is to ensure that health care billing is for the right amount, the right service, the right provider, and the right beneficiary. In addition to the MIP, CMS established four strategies to reduce payment errors:

- Effective program enrollment and education;
- Medical review and data analysis for early detection;
- Close cooperation with its partners such as Quality Improvement Organizations, the Office of Inspector General, the Federal Bureau of Investigation, the Department of Justice, as well as its contractors and providers; and
- Enforcement of policy.

Examples of fraud include altering records — claim forms or medical records — to receive higher payments, filing duplicate claims, unbundling, and outright billing for services not provided.

Abuse

Abuse differs from fraud in intent. An unintentional mistake, depending on the situation, is unlikely to constitute fraud but it can constitute abuse. Abuse does not need to meet the knowingly, willfully, and intentionality threshold of fraud. *Abuse* is typically defined as a mistake that results in unnecessary costs to any health care benefit program. When payment is made in situations where there is no legal entitlement to payment, abuse exists. Examples of abuse are charging in excess for services, providing services that do not meet professional standards, billing Medicare for services that are the responsibility of another carrier, not accepting assignment, and providing unnecessary medical services. In short, receiving unauthorized payment is abuse.

Lack of knowledge by members of an organization is no excuse. Therefore, medical office insurance staff members must be educated about the rules and regulations pertaining to medical insurance, and they must be trained to deal with the nuances in health care insurance billing. The detrimental effect on a medical practice of the allegation of fraud or abuse cannot be overstated.

FILING CLAIMS

Sending claims out the door (the act of actually filing a claim) may be one of the most straightforward processes medical office insurance staff members deal with in the course of their day. However, three issues come into play that can affect how quickly those claims are paid: the actions of clearinghouses, timely filing limits, and claim accuracy.

Clearinghouses

It should not be assumed that just because claims are sent from a medical practice, they have reached the insurance carrier for the claim to be paid. The role of a clearinghouse, either public or private, is to provide an interface for claims management. Clearinghouses receive claims from a practice management system by an interface and move that information to the appropriate payers, both government and commercial. In the role of facilitating claims processing, clearinghouses may receive information containing nonstandard elements in a nonstandard format and move that information into a format that will be acceptable to the payer intended to pay the claim. The reverse may also be true: standard transactions received by the clearinghouse may be put into a nonstandard format for the receiving organization.

The official definition of a health care clearinghouse can be found in the Department of Health and Human Services final HIPAA Privacy Rule in Section 160.103. Clearinghouses, like health care providers and health plans, are governed under the Privacy Rule. Clearinghouses operate with providers and health plans on a business-to-business level and do not deal directly with individual patients.

Clearinghouses typically use decision-support tools to validate that claims are clean in regard to completeness and accuracy so that they are correct when submitted to the payer. Not all clearinghouses are alike. Clearinghouses vary in their commitment to the provider and in their ability to deliver high-quality services to providers. Some clearinghouses have high claims acceptance rates and good editing processes with short time frames for reviewing claims for billing conflicts. Clearinghouses are good business associates if they are able to provide the medical practice with ease in viewing, editing, correcting, and submitting claims. Clearinghouses may prove to be costly business associates for the medical practice if they do not have good editing processes and do not report information to the medical practice in a timely manner. Months after a set of claims has left the medical practice, clearinghouses have been known to report back to the medical practice that the claims sent were not received by the carrier. Clearinghouses should be selected carefully. Agreements should be entered into only after a complete due diligence process is conducted.

Timely Filing

The issue of timely filing reinforces the importance of selecting a clearinghouse that will be a good business associate. *Timely filing* refers to the concept of requiring that claims be filed within a certain period of time from the date the service was provided. This concept typically favors insurance carriers rather than providers. It is common for commercial carriers to require that claims be filed within 90 days from the date of service. There are many unusual reasons that may arise in a medical practice that could delay a claim and cause it to miss the 90-day timely filing limit. Fortunately, these occasions are rare. Nevertheless, provider organizations are not benefited by this short time frame.

The Medicare fee-for-service regulation differs for timely filing. Medicare claims must be filed on or before December 31 of the calendar year following the year in which the service was delivered. An exception is made for those services furnished in the last three months of the calendar year; these claims are considered to be provided in the subsequent year and must be filed by December 31 of the following calendar year. For example, if a service is provided in July, the claim must be filed by December 31 of the following calendar year (17 months later). If a service is provided in November, Medicare considers that service to be provided in the following calendar year and the claim must be filed by December 31 of the next calendar year (25 months later). Services provided in October allow for the longest timely filing period (26 months). Medicare determines timely filing by comparing the date the service was furnished — the "from" date — to the receipt date to see if the timely filing requirement has been met. If not, the claim is denied with no opportunity for appeal, and the beneficiary may not be charged except for his or her deductible and coinsurance. A claim denied for timely filing reasons will have denial messages such as, "Reason code 29: The time limit for filing has expired." and "Remark code N211 — You may not appeal this decision." Exhibit 4.2 is adapted from CMS data and provides information to assist in tracking timely filing.[2]

Organizations that file claims in a timely fashion should never have to concern themselves with timely filing limits. Claims that are promptly filed are generally promptly paid. Organizations should strive to meet the best practice standard to file claims in a timely manner. Most E/M claims should be filed the day after the date of service. Even claims for procedures should be filed in a short

EXHIBIT 4.2 ■ Medicare Timely Filing Table

Date of Service	Months to File	Dec. 31 of service year, plus
January	23	1 year
February	22	1 year
March	21	1 year
April	20	1 year
May	19	1 year
June	18	1 year
July	17	1 year
August	16	1 year
September	15	1 year
October	26	1 year
November	25	1 year
December	24	1 year

Adapted from Centers for Medicare & Medicaid Services, "Chapter 1, General Billing Requirements," in Medicare Claims Processing Manual. Available online at www.cms.hhs.gov/transmittals/downloads/R830CP.pdf.

time frame. Unless timely filing is the standard for the organization, it cannot expect to maximize reimbursement from insurance carriers. In addition, staff members may expend more energy than usual collecting coinsurance on services when patients have already forgotten that they received those services.

Accuracy

The importance of accuracy in billing and filing claims cannot be overstated. When a service is accurately billed and filed in a timely manner, competent carriers will pay the service. Generally, issues that are ongoing are based on incompetence either on the part of the medical group or the carrier. Making sure that the medical group doesn't generate those issues usually falls to insurance staff members. They are in the best position to know what is being paid and what is being denied, and they must raise any related issues so that they may be corrected within the medical group. Otherwise, the medical group will continue to perpetuate its mistakes, reimbursement will fall short, and the entire organization will suffer.

Likewise, medical office insurance staff members must bring to the attention of administration the constant errors of carriers. Unfortunately, few medical office insurance departments have the clout that is needed to bring to bear the consequences that will effect change on the part of carriers. If accuracy is a pre-eminent goal of a medical practice, beginning with all medical office insurance staff members, and including their supervisors, administrators, and providers, the medical practice can avoid drowning in uncollected reimbursement for services provided in good faith.

PAYMENT POSTING

There are two critical pieces to payment posting: it must be timely and it must be accurate. Certainly, filing electronic claims daily is essential to the medical practice; so is daily payment posting. Optimally, all payments received by the medical practice should be posted the day they are received.

While not all organizations follow this model, it is the prudent model to implement as policy for many reasons. First, the time value of money is significant to all medical practices. Any revenue should be accessible to the practice as soon as it is available. Second, from a good business practice standard, money or checks should not be retained in the medical practice, as holding money or checks can invite problems. Medical practice organizations should have a policy defining their own threshold of reasonableness that lays out expectations relating to payment posting for current and future employees. Once the criteria relating to payment posting is established, employees must be held to executing the expected process. In many organizations, this important aspect of the revenue cycle is delayed by staff members who postpone payment posting due to the pressure of attending to other work responsibilities.

There are two ways a payment may be posted to the medical practice's account: manually or electronically with electronic funds transfer. Manual payment posting is labor intensive and expensive to the medical practice. It is fraught with human error and should be avoided. Payment posting, like all other aspects of the medical office insurance department, should rely on technology as much as possible. Moving away from manual posting to electronic posting with electronic funds transfer from the carrier is a good option whenever possible. Electronic posting and electronic funds transfer can help organizations manage the volume of paperwork that is inherent in the system. Also, using Medicare's electronic posting can give billing departments an opportunity to improve productivity.

In addition to having quicker access to funds and improved processing accuracy, the electronic approach should assist the medical office insurance department in retrieving information for account follow-up. For example, because patient information is already in electronic format, it is not necessary for insurance staff employees to scan EOBs for future retrieval when following up on the account. Anything that can be done in the organization to guarantee that payment posting is occurring accurately and quickly will improve the opportunity to have successful account follow-up.

As mentioned earlier, payment posting is an important aspect of the revenue cycle. It is also the point in time when payments should be audited for correctness. As each check is posted, payment amounts should be critically reviewed to ensure the correct amount was paid by the insurance carrier. Generally, mistakes are noticed if a payment is lower than it should be. The insurance carrier has little motivation to make correcting these problems their priority. Knowing that insurance carriers are paying the contracted amount per CPT code is easier if each carrier's contracted fee schedule is loaded into the practice management system. Efficient ways of loading carriers' fee schedules should be explored with practice management system vendors. Tracking and appealing payment discrepancies is essential to guarantee that the carrier is paying correctly; if it isn't, the loss of income for the medical practice can be significant over time. It is the responsibility of insurance staff members to manage denials aggressively so that revenue is not lost.

ACCOUNT FOLLOW-UP

It is essential that an organization establish a system for account follow-up. The system should be communicated in such a way that all members of the insurance department, both current employees and new hires, are aware of organizational expectations. Written processes or decision trees for account follow-up are helpful reminders to staff. Staff members should understand the processes within the system and internalize the reasoning behind each process. Understanding and internalization of processes will ensure that the organization's goals are passed on to new employees coming into the department. Developing a system takes some investment of time and input from management but is well worth the effort in terms of the positive results produced.

In the following section, processes for prioritizing work, handling rejections and denials, as well as the appeals process are discussed. For further information, the Medical Group Management Association (MGMA) has many excellent resources on account follow-up.

Prioritizing Work

Prioritizing work should be an organizational decision; it should not be left up to the discretion of staff members. An organized approach to working accounts receivable aging should be designated to staff members, and staff members should be held accountable for results. Possible approaches are to prioritize work based on carriers, physicians, or by aging buckets. Limitations or capabilities of practice management systems may play a role in dictating the best approach in an organization.

Some organizations favor having staff members specialize in working claims from a particular carrier. This approach assumes that learning the processes of various carriers streamlines operations and creates an advantage toward increasing efficiency. Other organizations create the impression of a small organization within a large organization, or a multispecialty organization, by assigning account follow-up to staff members per physician. While this can give staff members an opportunity to specialize in the follow-up for particular specialties, it may be a disadvantage for specific physicians if the insurance staff members assigned to their accounts are not as efficient and effective as other staff members.

On the other hand, some organizations assign follow-up work to insurance staff members by aging buckets using the traditional 30+, 60+, 90+, 120+, 150+, 180+ days categories. Organizations intent on achieving best practice status may conduct follow-up on accounts even before they rotate into the 30+ day bucket. These organizations have learned that attacking account follow-up sooner rather than later gives them a better opportunity to deal with the rejections, denials, and appeals processes within the time limits set by carriers so that getting paid for services is possible.

Rejections and Denials

Many rejection/denial determinations from carriers are based on the benefit structure of the insurance policy. Denials from carriers because of pre-existing conditions, because services or procedures are considered not medically necessary, or because conditions are not covered are almost impossible for the insurance department to preempt. Only the prior authorization process makes information known that will likely result in a denial from the insurance carrier to cover services.

The difficulty of insurance follow-up is compounded because most patients do not understand what is covered by their policies and what is not. Once again, these situations point to the necessity of gathering and retaining accurate patient information. If insurance staff members have accurate contact information for their patients, the insurance staff can contact patients so that they become involved early in the insurance payment process when there is a problem. The insured may be able to assist in clarifying with their human resources departments or with their insurance carriers the terms and conditions of their policies. Early contact with patients provides better understanding about the limitations of their insurance policies and sets the stage for them to accept financial responsibility for the services.

Many denials are corrected by minor adjustments to the insurance claim. Most of these issues are a result of human error on the part of medical practice employees that range from physicians to data entry staff. The organization is well served to discover these claims errors before the claims are filed. Large organizations try to correct minor issues by using claims scrubbers. While this process may not be financially viable for small organizations, it may be necessary for small organizations to use staff to utilize a manual process of verifying that information is accurately entered into the practice management system before claims are filed. Some small organizations that are already too tightly staffed may ignore the process of auditing information prior to the claim leaving the practice. This decision may prove to be more costly in the long run than making accommodations to verify accurate information before the claim leaves the practice. To reiterate from the discussion of clearinghouses earlier in this chapter, this is a task that differentiates a mediocre clearinghouse from a valuable one. Regardless of the process, medical office insurance staff members must work rejections/denials to resolve the account. It is well known that many payment denials are not resolved favorably for the medical practice. Resolution of the account often means filing an appeal.

Appeals

Medical office insurance staff members must familiarize themselves with the appeal process of the various carriers so that the practice has a better chance of winning an appeal for themselves and for their patient. Insurance staff should be aware that there are national organizations as well as state regulations and federal mandates relating to the appeals process when health insurance claims are denied. For example, the National Committee for Quality Assurance (NCQA) dictates that both physicians and health plans review appeals based on previous denials for payment of services. NCQA requires health plans to provide an opportunity for appeals review. After the internal appeal process has been exhausted, NCQA also requires that health plans allow for an external review process.

State departments of insurance are also important to the appeals process. Although state regulations may vary, typical state regulations provide that physicians have the right to advocate for appropriate medical care for patients and, therefore, allow physicians to have a role in determining medical necessity. States may also provide assistance to help patients with insurance appeals.

Federal mandates require all federal insurance programs as well as health plans that contract with Medicare to follow the processes for appeals recommended in the Consumer Bill of Rights and Responsibilities that was compiled by the Advisory Commission on Consumer Protection and Quality in the Health Care Industry (www.hcqualitycommission.gov).

Medicare Appeals Process

The Medicare appeals process for original, fee-for-service Medicare considers appeals at five different progressive levels: (1) redetermination; (2) reconsideration; (3) hearing by an administrative law judge (ALJ) in the Office of Medicare Hearings and Appeals; (4) review by the Medicare Appeals Council; and (5) judicial review in a federal district court. After an initial determination is made on a Medicare claim, appeals on both coverage and payment decisions can be made by beneficiaries, providers, or suppliers.

The first level of appeal in the Medicare appeals process is a redetermination that is filed in writing to the Medicare contractor using Form CMS-20027. Medicare contractors may also provide an online form to the medical practice for filing appeals. In such cases it is best to follow the appeal method preferred by the Medicare-contracted carrier in order to facilitate a quick response. The appeal must be filed within 120 days from the receipt of the initial determination, and any supporting documentation should be addressed. The medical administrative contractor (MAC) will typically issue a decision within 60 days.

The appeal for redetermination may be filed without regard to meeting a monetary threshold.

The second level of appeal may be filed if you disagree with the redetermination. The level of appeal is referred to as a reconsideration by a qualified independent contractor (QIC). The appeal must be filed with the QIC within 180 days of receiving the redetermination. The reconsideration request can be filed following the instructions on the Medicare Redetermination Notice (MRN) and can be filed on Form CMS-20033 that accompanies the MRN. The reconsideration request must provide and explain the evidence that supports disagreeing with the first level of appeal. At this level of appeal it is not necessary to resubmit information that has already been submitted to the contractor. The QIC will typically respond within 60 days from the request for consideration.

The right to a third level of appeal exists if the QIC cannot provide a decision that is fully favorable and within the applicable time frame. A monetary threshold of $120 must remain in controversy in order to request an ALJ hearing. This request must be made within 60 days from the QIC reconsideration decision. Using Form CMS-20034 A/B, practices can make a request for a hearing with an ALJ. At this level and subsequent levels of appeal, it is important to submit all information that should be considered in decision making. The ALJ will typically issue a determination within 90 days, but the decision make take longer based on the availability of all necessary information.

The fourth level of appeal applies if there is dissatisfaction with the ALJ's decision. A request for review by the Medicare Appeals Council must be submitted in writing within 60 days of the ALJ's decision. The ALJ's response will contain information about how to move to the fourth level of appeal. There is no monetary threshold at this level, but the appeal must be specific about the issues and prior findings being contested. Typically the Medicare Appeals Council will make a decision within 90 days.

Filing a request for a judicial review before a federal district court judge is the fifth and final level of appeal. This level requires that a substantial amount of money be in controversy. (In 2009 this amount was $1,220.[3]) The amount is increased annually based on a percentage of the consumer price index component for medical care and can be found on the CMS Website. This hearing must be requested within 60 days from the Medicare Appeals Council's determination.

Reopening a Claim

"Reopening" a claim is similar to an appeal. A reopening can occur because of an overpayment or an underpayment. The primary difference between a reopening and an appeal is the initiating party. Medicare contractors take action to reopen a determination. While a provider can initiate reopening, the decision to reopen is at the discretion of the Medicare contractor. On the other hand, the right to appeal is mandatory. Typically a provider can request a reopening if there is a minor clerical error, but, if the provider disagrees with the decision relating to a claim, an appeal should be filed.

CORRESPONDENCE

The professionalism of the medical practice is reflected by the correspondence it generates. The quality of correspondence either reflects well or poorly on the physicians. All written correspondence should be set in a business format, use good grammar with correct spelling, and contain clear, concise language. As much as is practical, staff members should use templates for correspondence. However, it should not appear to be a copy of a copy (an unprofessional look can be avoided by scanning originals into copy machines or using computer templates).

Insurance Carriers

Correspondence with insurance carriers can be both verbal and written. Medical office insurance staff members do much of their work talking on the telephone to resolve issues. That type of verbal communication is inevitable in the course of resolving accounts. Because verbal communication is so critical, it is important for medical office insurance staff members to develop good verbal skills. Staff members realize that the art of asking the right question at the right time can be essential to moving the claims process toward resolution.

Written communication to insurance carriers is no less important. All types of written communication to insurance carriers should be well thought through by staff and management so that templates can be developed and established for use by all staff members. Standardized templates within the organization can save time for busy staff and can be more apt to convey the appropriate message to resolve the issue at hand. Sample letters, indexed by problem type, saved in a computer file to be accessed by all staff members is optimal.

It is also necessary for insurance staff to have ready access to the terms of the contract held by the medical practice with various insurance carriers. Contracts can be scanned for easy access. Management or lead insurance staff members can create summary documents for the entire staff to use. These summary documents should outline the major points of insurance contracts and list the carriers' contact information. An investment of time and energy at the time of contracting can have major payoffs when communicating with insurance carriers.

Patients

Like correspondence with insurance carriers, correspondence with patients will be both verbal and written. Patients are often confused about communication relating to their health care. They might wonder whether the communication really relates to them if it has a name listed as the provider other than the name of their physician. Particularly when patients have diagnostic testing, often they are surprised to receive a bill for services from someone other than their doctor. Patients in our society have heard many horrendous stories in the popular media about negative aspects of health care. This climate has made them suspicious and distrustful about the health care industry. It is extremely important to the medical practice that insurance staff members present the practice as a competent, helpful, and empathetic organization even when they are serious about collecting for services provided.

Insurance staff members should be familiar with every piece of financial communication that goes out to patients so that they can identify the communication piece that patients are speaking about when they call insurance staff. Insurance staff members should be acquainted with the format of statements. Often medical practices send out statements that are so difficult to read that even individuals working in the organization are not able to understand the information. Insurance staff should be able to read a statement sent out by the organization and readily help the patient interpret what the information on the statement means. Insurance staff also should be able to look at their practice management screen and track the information that is on the patient's statement. The explanation staff members give regarding charges and balances that are due will incline patients to pay sooner or delay payment. In general, when giving explanation to patients, individuals working in health care should be careful to use language that patients can understand rather than jargon that is common only to those working in the health care industry. Staff members should make certain that their communication with patients gives the patient the impression that the staff member is friendly, fair, and informed.

MGMA, in conjunction with the Healthcare Financial Management Association and the American Hospital Association, have developed and articulated a "Patient Friendly Billing" philosophy. Patient Friendly Billing outlines voluntary standards designed to communicate better with patients when conveying financial information. Patient Friendly Billing states that the communication should be "clear, concise, and correct." This philosophy asserts that following that simple principle will help produce many benefits such as better patient satisfaction, fewer financial questions from patients, and patients paying their portion of the service faster. (More information regarding Patient Friendly Billing can be found at www.mgma.com.)

COLLECTIONS

"Collections" is a sensitive topic in many medical practices. Turning patients' account balances over to a collections agency may be even more sensitive. Each organization must develop a philosophy relating to how it deals with account balances it is unable to collect. If medical practices make a conscious effort to increase standards in every aspect of the practice, including better performance with greater accuracy in billing, one can only hope that patients who can pay will be more apt to pay. Most medical practices today find that it is necessary to use an outside collection agency for those accounts that they are unable to collect. Clearly, it serves the practice well to keep that number to a minimum. Increasing efficiencies inside the organization is a better investment in the long run than paying an outside agency.

Credit Balances

Medical practices should be as diligent about refunding money to patients as they are about collecting money from patients. Credit balances on account in the medical practice can result from many different situations. Money can be owed to carriers or to patients. A quick turnaround in sending patient refunds builds goodwill with patients and reinforces the impression that the medical practice is efficient and effective. If patients can trust the medical practice both to provide good care and to be reliable in financial matters, they will choose that practice when they need care in the future for themselves and their family.

Offsets

When carriers have overpaid, they often compensate by making an adjustment in future payments. These offsets or "recoups" are legitimate and give the carriers an opportunity to compensate themselves for money due from the practice. Medical practices should exercise care when dealing with amounts that the carrier reports as an overpayment. Sometimes the communication coming from the carrier indicates that the medical practice is to refund the overpayment, but the practice of the carrier may be to recoup the overpayment by deducting the amount overpaid from the next check sent to the practice. These situations are difficult to resolve and can become a lengthy process. While it is right for the carrier who overpaid to recover the overpayment, it is not a good use of the practice's resources to try to recover the income for services a second time. Staff members who know the working habits of carriers can help formulate policy within the organization about which carriers they refund and under what circumstances as opposed to those carriers they know will recoup money.

References

1. Centers for Medicare & Medicaid Services, *The 1997 Documentation Guidelines for Evaluation and Management Services*. Available online at www.cms.hhs.gov/MLNProducts/Downloads/MASTER1.pdf. Accessed 3/13/09.

2. Centers for Medicare & Medicaid Services, "Chapter 1, General Billing Requirements," in *Medicare Claims Processing Manual*. Available online at www.cms.hhs.gov/transmittals/downloads/R830CP.pdf. Accessed 3/13/09.

3. *Federal Register*, Vol. 73, No. 188, Friday, Sept. 26, 2008/Notices, page 55847.

CHAPTER FIVE

Scenarios

Medical office insurance staff members face difficult situations every day in the course of doing their work. The situations are not always straightforward. Most situations require staff members to have both broad knowledge and good problem-solving skills to be able to handle them well. It is important for staff members to represent the medical practice well so that patients don't lose confidence in the organization. Staff members can be taught how to handle situations and how to transfer knowledge from one situation to another.

The following scenarios provide real life examples of the kinds of situations medical office insurance staff members may face in the course of their work. These scenarios can help to give staff members confirmation of the best way to handle difficult situations and instill confidence about how to handle similar situations in the future. Reviewing these scenarios with potential staff members can also provide managers an opportunity to judge the knowledge and problem-solving skills a new hire might bring to the organization.

SCENARIO 1

The Always Best Care (ABC) medical practice has determined that it will apply the National Correct Coding Initiative (CCI) to all claim situations, including claims for both participating and non-participating carriers. This decision has been made so that everyone is in the habit of abiding by the CCI and to ensure that Medicare claims are always in compliance with the CCI. Mary, one of ABC's patients, has American Health Care, a commercial insurance carrier. ABC is not contracted with American Health Care. Mary had three lesions removed by Dr. Jones at the ABC medical practice. When American Health Care paid for the service it paid the first lesion at 80 percent of the standard charge. Each of the other two lesions was paid at 80 percent of half the standard charge. The explanation of benefits (EOB) listed the remainder of the charge as the patient's responsibility. How will the balance on these charges be handled?

a. Mary will be billed for the balance on the charges as listed on the EOB.

b. Insurance staff will write off 50 percent of the charge for the second and third lesion and Mary will be responsible for the remaining 20 percent that American Health Care did not pay.

c. Insurance staff will call the insurance carrier and find out why it paid 80 percent of half the charge on the second and third lesions.

d. c then a.

The best answer is b. Insurance staff will post 80 percent payment on the first lesion and the second and third lesions will be reduced by 50 percent based on the CCI and the 80 percent payment posted. Mary will be billed for her co-insurance of 20 percent on the first lesion and 20 percent of half the charge on both the second and third lesions.

SCENARIO 2

Pam's insurance is state Medicaid. This state requires a second opinion before it will pay for a procedure. Pam is a patient of Always Best Care medical practice and was seen 14 months ago for gallbladder disease by Dr. Wilson. After her last visit she did not follow up to schedule a second opinion for surgery. Now she has called with the same problem. She has asked to be appointed with Dr. Smith and is scheduled to see him on Monday. She has told Dr. Smith's nurse that after she sees Dr. Smith she wants to schedule her surgery to be done by the end of the week because she is already scheduled off work. Dr. Smith's nurse has asked Amy, who works in the insurance department, if this is okay. What should Amy tell Dr. Smith's nurse must happen for Medicaid to pay for the surgery?

a. Medicaid will pay for the surgery because Dr. Smith may be considered the second opinion because the problem is the same.

b. Mary needs to see another physician for a second opinion before her surgery for Medicaid to pay.

c. Mary can only have Dr. Wilson do the surgery because he was the first doctor she saw.

d. Mary is required to wait one year to get a second opinion.

The best answer is b. Mary needs a second opinion before Medicaid will pay for the surgery. Mary's visit to Dr. Wilson was too long ago for it to be considered as the first opinion and Dr. Smith to be the second opinion. Unless Dr. Smith's nurse can work Mary in with another physician this week for a second opinion, Mary will likely not be able to have her surgery this week even though she has already scheduled off work.

SCENARIO 3

The Always Best Care medical practice posts all insurance payments based on the date of service listed on the explanation of benefits (EOB) as the date of service rendered. Mary, a patient of the medical practice, paid by check for her co-insurance. She wrote her check for $88.00. Her coinsurance as stated on the EOB from American Health Care was $58.00. Mary has an old balance owed to the group of $70.00 in a personal pay status. What is the most prudent application of the $88.00 that Mary paid?

a. The money should be refunded to Mary because the coinsurance was only $58.00.

b. The money should be sent back to the insurance carrier.

c. The money can be applied to her old personal pay balance.

d. Mary should be called to see what she wants done with the money.

The best answer is c. Medical practices are under no obligation to apply a personal payment to any certain charge. Based on the policy of the medical practice, it is a good practice to get the oldest balances paid off first. The money should be applied to her old personal balance of $70.00 and the $18.00 applied to the coinsurance for the recent service. Again based on organizational policy, it would be good public relations to call Mary and explain to her how her payment was applied.

SCENARIO 4

Bill, a patient of Always Best Care medical practice, received services from Dr. Jones last month. When a member of the insurance staff from the practice asked Bill's commercial insurance carrier when Dr. Jones can expect payment on the service, insurance staff received information from Bill's carrier that it is waiting to get additional information from Bill before paying on the service. What should Ann, who is working insurance for Dr. Jones, do in this situation?

a. Wait for Bill to fill out the form his insurance carrier needs.

b. Call Bill to advise him that Dr. Jones will not be paid until he completes and sends the form back to his insurance carrier.

c. Call Bill to advise him that Dr. Jones will not be paid until he completes and sends the form back to his insurance carrier. Ann may instruct Bill that if he does not comply with his carrier's request, the carrier will deny payment on the claim and the balance on the service will be transferred to a personal pay balance.

d. Call the carrier.

The best answer is c. The insurance carrier will not pay Dr. Jones until Bill fills out the form and sends it back to the carrier. The insurance carrier may be inquiring about a pre-existing condition, a work-related accident, an injury, or other insurance coverage. Sometimes the only leverage to make sure that the patient complies with the wishes of the carrier is to let the patient know that if the carrier denies payment, the balance will be moved to a personal pay balance.

SCENARIO 5

Mary works for a surgical group. Dr. Little was called to consult on a patient in a long-term acute care (LTAC) hospital. Dr. Little made the determination that the patient needed an amputation. The LTAC hospital has made arrangements to send the patient to another hospital that had operating room facilities that will better be able to serve the patient's needs. Dr. Little did the procedure in the hospital to which the patient was transferred. The service was billed to Medicare. Medicare denied payment on the service saying that the patient was an inpatient at another facility on the date of service. How will Mary get payment for Dr. Little?

  a. Appeal the claim to Medicare and if it denies the claim again, bill the patient.
  b. Tell Dr. Little that he will not get paid because he didn't do a discharge summary from the LTAC hospital and then readmit the patient after the amputation.
  c. Turn to the LTAC hospital for payment.
  d. Turn to the hospital where the procedure was done for payment.

The best answer is c. Medicare will not pay the claim even if it is appealed and the patient cannot be billed. Dr. Little could not have discharged the patient from the LTAC hospital before doing the procedure because the patient could not have been admitted back to the LTAC hospital after the procedure because of Interruption of Stay regulations. The only place Dr. Little can turn for payment is the LTAC hospital. Whether Dr. Little will be paid by the LTAC hospital depends on how much his services may be needed by the LTAC hospital in the future. The LTAC hospital is under no obligation to pay Dr. Little for this service if he did not have a service agreement signed with the LTAC hospital. Medicare Part A pays the LTAC hospital whereas Medicare Part B would normally pay Dr. Little.

SCENARIO 6

Mrs. Jones has been a regular patient of Dr. Barkley, seeing him for her yearly check-ups. Dr. Barkley has left the practice and has moved to another state. Dr. James, who was formerly a partner of Dr. Barkley's, is seeing Mrs. Jones today. Dr. James's nurse has called the front desk to correct the appointment schedule. She tells Julie, the receptionist, that Mrs. Jones is a new patient because this is the first time she has seen Dr. James. Julie has called Barb in the insurance department to verify that Mrs. Jones is a new patient. What does Barb tell Julie?

  a. Yes, Mrs. Jones is a new patient and the visit should be charged as a new patient.
  b. No, Mrs. Jones is not a new patient.
  c. Yes, Mrs. Jones is a new patient because Dr. Barkley has moved out of state.

d. Yes, she is a new patient because Julie has told Barb that she is afraid Dr. James will get angry and not see her if she is not listed as a new patient.

The correct answer is b. Mrs. Jones is a new patient to the medical practice if she has not been seen in the practice for three years. The fact that it is the first time Dr. James is seeing Mrs. Jones has no bearing on her status as an established patient in the practice. It is not relevant to the situation that Dr. Barkley moved out of state.

SCENARIO 7

Mary tells Jane that she will pay a down payment on her deductible from her flexible spending account (FSA) for the surgery she is scheduled to have with Dr. Reynolds. Mary reports that she is glad that she is having the surgery in January because she did not spend all of the money in her FSA last year. Jane inquires further and learns that Mary is not participating in the FSA that her employer has established this year because she had $500.00 left in her FSA from the last calendar year. Will Mary's FSA provide the money for Mary to pay for the January deductible?

a. Yes, any money not used will be carried over to the first quarter of the next calendar year.

b. Yes, it is Mary's money and she can use it as she wants.

c. No, Mary must spend the money for services that are provided in the calendar year for which the money was designated.

d. No, Mary must use FSA money in the month that the money is held out of her payroll check.

The correct answer is c. Flexible spending accounts are set up by employers for a calendar year. Unless an employee uses the money for services that are provided during the calendar year in which the money was deferred, the employee forfeits the money.

SCENARIO 8

Mary works for Great Patient Care medical practice. The practice put in a new practice management system last year, and since then staff members have been having problems with claims. Mr. Smith, a patient of the medical practice, has just called saying that he was told by Medicare that Medicare will not be paying the doctor in the group for the services provided to him. Mr. Smith says that the doctor saved his life and he wants him to be paid, but he cannot afford to pay for the services. He asked Mary to appeal the decision. She followed up on the phone call and discovered that Medicare did not pay the claim because the timely filing limit was not met by her organization. Mary must call Mr. Smith back to let him know what she has learned. What does she tell Mr. Smith?

a. That she will appeal the claim.

b. That he will be responsible for the payment that should have been paid by Medicare.

c. That often the initial determination by Medicare is wrong and she will re-file the claim.

d. That Mr. Smith is not responsible for paying for the services except for his deductible, if not met, and coinsurance.

The best answer is d. The timely filing decision is not an initial determination. When the claim is denied because the timely filing limit has not been met, there is no opportunity for appeal. When a claim has been denied because of timely filing, the physician may collect only the deductible and coinsurance from the patient.

SCENARIO 9

Dr. Anderson saw Mr. Camp in the medical practice on April 1 and removed a large lesion from his back. Mr. Camp saw Dr. Anderson in the medical practice again on April 11 for a problem relating to the lesion removal. How is Mr. Camp charged?

a. He will be charged an Evaluation and Management (E/M) code based on what the doctor does.

b. He will not be charged because his visit is within the postoperative period.

c. He will be charged an E/M code using modifier 57.

d. He will not be charged because he is within the 90-day postoperative period.

The correct answer is b. Minor procedures have a 10-day postoperative period — the day of the surgery is counted with 10 follow-up days. Major surgeries have a 90-day postoperative period. Modifier 57 is the decision for surgery modifier.

SCENARIO 10

Dr. Anderson reviewed his charges and told Jill's supervisor that Jill, a member of the medical practice's insurance staff, should have charged an Evaluation and Management (E/M) visit code in addition to the procedure code for the lesion he removed from Mr. Camp's back on April 1. Jill's supervisor asked Jill why she didn't charge a visit code and to add the visit code charge. How should Jill handle this situation?

a. Add the E/M code on the April 1 charge along with the procedure.

b. Add modifier 59 to the procedure on April 1.

c. Explain that for minor procedures the visit code is always included and not billed separately.

d. Add modifier 57 because Dr. Anderson decided to take the lesion off the day that Mr. Camp was in the office for his physical exam.

The correct answer is c. For minor procedures, the initial visit (consultation or evaluation) is always included and not billed separately. Modifier 59 is used to signify a separate or different procedure and is not used with an E/M code. Modifier 57 is the decision for surgery modifier.

SCENARIO 11

Jill's supervisor came back to Jill and told her that Dr. Anderson wants to charge the E/M code in addition to the lesion he removed from Mr. Camp's back because the lesion was so large and complicated to excise. What information can Jill give her supervisor that can help Dr. Anderson?

  a. Add modifier 22 to the procedure charge code.

  b. Add modifier 78 to the procedure charge code.

  c. Add modifier 58 to the procedure charge code.

  d. Add modifiers 78 and 58 to the procedure charge code.

The correct answer is a. In the Excision—Benign Lesions section of the Current Procedural Terminology (CPT®)* codebook, the reader is instructed to add modifier 22 for unusual or complicated excisions. Modifier 78 is used for a return trip to the operating room for complications. Modifier 58 is used for planned staging of procedures.

SCENARIO 12

The Always Best Care (ABC) medical practice has all of its new patients sign a form that it calls Signature on File, Assignment of Benefits, & Financial Agreement. Mr. Cook came in for a visit with Dr. Foley and signed all of the new patient paperwork as the practice asked. Mr. Cook's insurance claim was filed but the carrier did not pay, saying that it did not cover the service provided. ABC's insurance department staff moved the charges to the personal pay category. Mr. Cook got his bill from ABC and called the practice saying that he is not responsible for the bill because he was not told by the practice that his insurance wouldn't cover the service provided. Is Mr. Cook personally responsible for the charges?

  a. No, it is the medical practice's responsibility to tell patients when their insurance does not cover the service provided.

  b. Yes, Mr. Cook took financial responsibility to pay ABC when he signed the form that said that if the services were not covered that he would be responsible for the charge.

  c. No, the medical practice cannot charge patients when they provide services that are risky and are not covered by the insurance carrier.

  d. Yes, Mr. Cook will be turned over for collections because he called in saying that he will not pay.

The correct answer is b. Mr. Cook took financial responsibility when he signed the financial agreement with ABC. The insurance department staff members should be familiar with the language in the new patient paperwork so that they can remind patients that they accepted financial responsibility. The medical practice cannot be responsible to know a patient's benefits package. The medical practice met its insurance obligation to Mr. Cook by correctly filing his claim to his insurance carrier.

SCENARIO 13

Mr. Smith works at a small appliance store that has eight employees. His employer has a group health plan and provides insurance coverage for Mr. Smith. Mr. Smith also has Medicare. Mr. Smith came to the Always Best Care medical practice to see Dr. Andrews. The last time Mr. Smith came to the practice he did not have Medicare. The front desk called the insurance department to see if his insurance needs to be updated. What does the insurance department tell the front desk staff person?

a. No, his insurance is the same.
b. Yes, Medicare should be added as the secondary payer.
c. Yes, Medicare should be made the primary payer and the group health plan is secondary payer.
d. No, Medicare won't pay as long as Mr. Smith is working.

The correct answer is c. If a patient has Medicare insurance and is covered by a group health plan by an employer who has less than 20 employees, Medicare is the primary payer and the group health plan is the secondary payer.

SCENARIO 14

Mrs. Jones is a disabled Medicare beneficiary. Her husband, Mr. Jones, works for a large chain store that has 800 employees. Mr. Jones and his wife have group health plan insurance coverage provided by his employer. Mrs. Jones came to Always Best Care medical practice to see Dr. Andrews. The last time Mrs. Jones was in the medical practice she only had Medicare. The front desk called the insurance department to see if her insurance needs to be updated. What does the insurance department tell the front desk staff person?

a. No, Medicare will pay because Mrs. Jones is disabled.
b. Yes, Medicare should be changed to the secondary insurance as the group health plan is now the primary insurance.
c. Yes, the group health plan should be added as a secondary insurance.
d. Yes, Medicare should be dropped and the group health plan should be added.

The correct answer is b. If a patient is a disabled Medicare beneficiary and is covered by a large group health plan of 100 or more employees, the large group health plan pays as the primary payer and Medicare pays as the secondary payer.

SCENARIO 15

Mr. Sawyer called Jeanette at Dr. Layton's office. His wife, Mrs. Sawyer, has Medicare Part A. She is also covered by Mr. Sawyer's group health plan. Dr. Layton did a procedure on Mrs. Sawyer in the hospital, which Dr. Layton scheduled as an inpatient procedure. The medical office billed the service as inpatient and Dr. Layton was paid by the group health plan. Now Mr. Sawyer is calling saying that Medicare won't pay the hospital stay because the hospital billed charges as if Mrs. Sawyer was an outpatient. How should Jeanette handle the situation?

   a. Tell Mr. Sawyer that she doesn't know what happened at the hospital.

   b. Tell Mr. Sawyer that Dr. Layton got paid and Mr. Sawyer will have to deal with the hospital himself.

   c. Tell Mr. Sawyer that she will call the hospital insurance staff and send them a copy of Dr. Layton's order for Mrs. Sawyer's procedure so that they will correct their billing.

   d. Tell Mr. Sawyer to tell the hospital that Medicare Part A paid Dr. Layton and that the hospital filed its claim incorrectly.

The correct answer is c. Medicare Part A will pay for inpatient stays at the hospital only. If Jeanette will send Dr. Layton's order to the hospital billing department, they can correct their billing and be paid by Medicare. Jeanette should act on the behalf of Dr. Layton's patient to try to straighten out the problem.

SCENARIO 16

Dr. Smith employs Mary. Mrs. Low is a patient of Dr. Smith. She trusts Dr. Smith and his organization. Because Mary files insurance claims for Dr. Smith's medical practice, Mrs. Low asks Mary's advice on which Medigap policy she should purchase as a supplement for her Medicare insurance. How might Mary handle this situation?

   a. Mary can say she is sorry that she can't help Mrs. Low.

   b. Mary can give Mrs. Low some of the Medigap policy carriers' names that she has had experience with as paying well.

   c. Mary can tell Mrs. Low that she should buy the policy her grand-mother has.

   d. Mary can tell her that she doesn't sell insurance.

The correct answer is b. It would be inappropriate for Mary to recommend a product outright, but she can share her experience with Mrs. Low. Patients have a relationship with their physician and their physician's staff members. They tend to transfer the trust they have for a provider to staff members and vice versa.

SCENARIO 17

Mrs. Blue is a patient of Dr. Smith. She has been in the hospital for three weeks. As has been the habit for three weeks, Dr. Smith dictated in his hospital charges that he visited Mrs. Blue on Monday. Again on Wednesday he dictated that he visited her in the hospital. On Tuesday, he forgot to dictate that he visited her. Mary, Dr. Smith's employee, is aware that he made rounds on his hospital patients on Tuesday. Mary has tried to catch Dr. Smith for two days to ask about the lack of dictation but has been unsuccessful. The weekly charges must go in today. How might Mary handle this situation?

    a. Mary can charge for the visit and have Dr. Smith dictate when she can catch him.

    b. Mary can leave a note for Dr. Smith to dictate and go ahead and get the charge in.

    c. Mary knows that Dr. Smith saw Mrs. Blue. She can charge.

    d. Mary will not meet the deadline to get that charge in today because she cannot catch Dr. Smith.

The correct answer is d. Dr. Smith, not Mary, is accountable for his charges. Mary cannot presume that Dr. Smith saw Mrs. Blue. She should wait for confirmation and charge when she can verify with Dr. Smith that he did see the patient on Tuesday. If Mary enters the charge without verification, she is overstepping her authority. Because she has tried for two days and cannot catch Dr. Smith, if she enters the charge on her own it is likely she will forget to verify the charge when she does see him.

SCENARIO 18

Mr. Jones, who lives alone and has no family, has recently been hospitalized. He has received statements from anesthesia, pathology, gastroenterology, and surgery. He has received an explanation of benefits (EOB) from Medicare and from his secondary insurance. Mr. Jones thinks that all of the paperwork he has received relates to bills to be paid. Susan works for Mr. Jones' family practice doctor. Mr. Jones has been a patient of the practice for years. He is a very nice man and brings candy to the staff every time he comes in the office. Mr. Jones has asked Susan to help him figure out his bills. How might Susan handle this situation?

    a. Susan tells Mr. Jones that she would be happy to help him because she knows that kind of patient service would be in keeping with the philosophy of her organization.

    b. Susan tells Mr. Jones that he will have to call Medicare to get answers.

    c. Susan tells Mr. Jones that he will need to go to each office and have each office pull out what charges relate to him.

    d. Susan gives Mr. Jones a Website to look up information about EOBs.

For most organizations the correct answer is a. Medical office insurance staff members know their organization's philosophy regarding helping patients work through the health care maze of insurance and EOBs. While organizations cannot afford to pay staff to waste time or spend an inordinate amount of time on any activity that is not generating revenue for the practice, it is appropriate to help patients in need. Some staff members suggested that they could have Mr. Jones come in before work or at noon so that the time they spend with him would not deter from their work time.

SCENARIO 19

A new CPT code has been published that exactly fits a procedure Julie's organization does frequently. The old CPT code was not exactly descriptive of the procedure, but Medicare paid on that code. Now, after four months, Medicare is still not paying on the new code. Medicare has rejected payment on every claim with the new CPT code. This amounts to a great deal of revenue for Julie's organization that is outstanding. How might Julie handle this situation?

    a. Julie bills the old code because it pays.

    b. Julie bills the correct code and works with her medicare administrative contractor (MAG) to get the new code paid.

    c. Julie calls her congressman.

    d. Julie holds all of the claims until Medicare starts paying on the new code.

The correct answer is b. Julie is required to use the correct code for billing purposes. Continuing to use the old code will result eventually in all of the claims needing to be filed again correctly. If she holds the claims with that code, she will not know when Medicare starts to pay on the correct code. She should bill the claims correctly and continue to work with her MAC to resolve the issue.

SCENARIO 20

Dr. Johnson charged a Level 4 Evaluation and Management code for seeing Mr. Rockford in the medical office. Mr. Rockford is a long-term patient, and Karen, Dr. Johnson's employee, is familiar with his treatment. In Dr. Johnson's dictation for the office visit, he only dictated one diagnosis. Karen knows that one diagnosis will not support a Level 4 charge. Dr. Johnson left out information relating to the complete diagnosis. He did not include that Mr. Rockford is on a blood thinner medication and has diabetes. How might Karen handle this situation?

    a. Karen asks Dr. Johnson to append the dictation before the service is billed, explaining why.

    b. This is not Karen's issue and she should not get involved.

    c. Karen goes back and adds the information to Dr. Johnson's dictation.

    d. Karen tells Mr. Rockford that Dr. Johnson is overcharging.

The correct answer is a. Karen cannot append the dictation herself; that would be overstepping her bounds. Karen is a member of the medical practice team and she should help any other member when she sees that she can. She can hold the charge until Dr. Johnson has an opportunity to append the dictation.

SCENARIO 21

Medicare has publicized for several months that new rules will go into effect April 1. Karen's organization has not made details regarding the new rules and regulations accessible to her. Karen's manager has been out because of sickness. It is now April 15, and Karen remembers the effective date of the new rules. Karen's experience has been that Medicare often postpones the implementation date of new rules and regulations, but she does not want her organization to violate Medicare's regulations. How might Karen handle this situation?

a. Karen can go to the Centers for Medicare & Medicaid (CMS) Website to see what she can find out about the new regulations.

b. Karen can go talk to her manager's superior to explain the situation and ask for advice.

c. Karen can call her local Medicare Administrative Contractor (MAC) to see if the regulations have been postponed.

d. All of the above.

The correct answer is d. Karen cannot put the organization at risk by not acting on something that she knows could become a problem. Calling the MAC and doing research on the CMS Website are both good options for Karen to educate herself. Even if implementation of processes to support new regulations is not Karen's responsibility, she should go to her manager's supervisor with as much information as possible about the situation so that a decision can be made for the organization.

SCENARIO 22

Medicare has publicized changes to rules that include contradictory information. Jill has attended two outside seminars relating to these changes. One seminar interpreted the changes differently than the other one. Jill has phoned the Medicare carrier. Jill has been given clarifying information over the phone; however, she forgot to clarify one issue and phoned Medicare a second time. This time she spoke with a different Medicare representative and was given information that conflicted with the first call. How might Jill handle this situation?

a. If Jill cannot find clarifying information on the Centers for Medicare & Medicaid (CMS) Website, she should call the Medicare Administrative Contractor again asking to speak to a supervisor to get clarification. She should ask for the information in writing.

b. Jill should follow the advice of the second seminar that had the most updated information.

c. Jill thinks that the first seminar was more credible and will follow their advice.

d. Jill should call Medicare the third time to see if she can get one of the answers again. Then she will go with the "two out of three" rule.

The correct answer is a. If Jill cannot find clarifying information on the CMS Website, she must call Medicare again to get the correct answer. The "best two out of three" approach is not advisable.

SCENARIO 23

Mr. Craw is 70 years old and injured his back while helping his friend move. His friend has liability insurance. Mr. Craw works for a packing plant and has group health plan insurance from his employer. He also has Medicare Part B health insurance. After Mr. Craw provided the medical office front desk staff with the liability insurance information, he phoned Jill in the medical practice's insurance department saying that he does not want the office to file with his friend's liability insurance. He turned the injury in to his employer as a workers' compensation injury but he does not yet have approval by his employer. He asked Jill to file the claim with workers' compensation. How might Jill handle this situation?

a. Jill should wait to see if the employer will say it is fine to file the claim with workers' compensation.

b. Jill can explain to Mr. Craw that when he saw the physician he explained how he hurt his back and that the details relating to his injury are in his medical chart.

c. Jill can explain to Mr. Craw that workers' compensation will request his records to verify the source of his injury. Once verified that the injury was not work related, workers' compensation insurance will not pay.

d. b and c.

The correct answer is d. Jill cannot participate in Mr. Craw's deception. Mr. Craw may not understand that he is asking for the medical practice to participate in insurance fraud. Regardless, the medical practice has the liability information, and liability insurance should be billed. Some staff members suggested that Mr. Craw should be given a pamphlet that explains insurance fraud.

SCENARIO 24

Mary works in the insurance department. The insurance department files claims daily, but because of intake mistakes made at the front desk, many claims are filed incorrectly. Every claim filed incorrectly doubles the workload of the insurance department staff. Management in Mary's organization expects insurance claims to be worked in a timely fashion; however, the workload in Mary's department can't possibly be managed with the number of staff employed. Mary has spoken to management about this situation, but no changes have been made. The front desk still makes many mistakes, and no new staff is added to the insurance department. Mary likes the people in the organization, and management does not seem to hold her responsible for the problem. How might Mary handle this situation?

    a. Mary should quit her job if nothing changes.

    b. Mary and her insurance colleagues should make an appointment with management to help them understand the situation.

    c. Mary can approach front desk personnel to see if there is anything they may need from the insurance department that would help them do their job better.

    d. All of the above.

The best answer is d. This scenario provides a picture of many insurance departments throughout the nation. Options b and c demonstrate that the insurance department staff is trying to be a part of the solution, and both options should be carried out without making accusations and assigning blame. Option a is a last-resort option. It is impossible to succeed in a medical office insurance department without support from management.

SCENARIO 25

Mr. Carr is 70 years old. He was adamant with the front desk staff that his medical services are to be billed to Medicare as the primary payer. He had no Medicare card to copy but gave the front desk staff a Medicare number that appears to be legitimate. Now his information has been sent to the insurance department. While reviewing his records, Karen notices that his last office visit charges were paid by a group health plan. After checking with Mr. Carr regarding his employer group health plan, he tells Karen that he retired last month. How might Karen handle this situation?

    a. Karen should bill the group health plan.

    b. Karen can call Mr. Carr's Medicare Coordination of Benefits (COB) contractor.

    c. Karen can call Mr. Carr and tell him that he needs to straighten this out himself.

    d. Karen can call Mr. Carr's former employer to see if Mr. Carr is on Medicare.

The best answer is b. Karen can call the Medicare COB contractor to verify whether Mr. Carr has benefits. The function of the COB is to identify if benefits exist that will put Medicare in a position to be the secondary payer. The role of COB is to make sure payment mistakes are not made.

Modifiers

Modifiers are the numeric codes that increase or decrease the relative value unit (RVU) of a Current Procedural Terminology (CPT®)* code. A complete list of CPT modifiers is found in the CPT codebook published by the American Medical Association. It is important for every medical office's billing department to have a current CPT codebook. The content of the book is updated yearly. The list of modifiers is found on the inside of the front cover of the CPT codebook, and broader definitions are found in Appendix A. Modifiers serve to notify that some special circumstance existed relating to the CPT code used to describe the procedure or service provided.

The following discussion addresses some situations that may cause confusion about how and when to use modifiers. Medicare instructs that if one is in doubt about using a certain modifier, one should contact the provider relations department at the local Medicare contractor.

The term *global surgical package* refers to the usual pre- and postoperative care pertaining to a particular CPT code for a surgical procedure. The usual pre- and postoperative care included in the global surgical package includes the pre-operative visits after the decision is made to operate, intra-operative services, management of complications following surgery, postoperative visits, post-surgical pain management from the surgeon, most supplies, and miscellaneous services relating to the surgery. Services that may be paid separate from global surgical packages include the initial patient evaluation, services of another physician other than in the transfer of surgical care, visits unrelated to the surgical procedure, diagnostic tests, distinct unrelated surgical procedures, return trips to the operating room, and a more extensive procedure.

Global surgical packages carry certain billing requirements. Major procedures have a 90-day postoperative period, which means the global period for major surgeries includes the day before the surgery, the day of the surgery, and 90 days following the surgery. Counting the postoperative period for minor surgeries differs. Minor procedures have a 10-day postoperative period, which means the day of the surgery is counted with 10 follow-up days. For minor procedures, the initial visit (consultation or evaluation) is always included and is not billed separately. If a procedure has 0, 10, or 90 postoperative days in a global period, modifier 22 can be billed to signify that the procedure was substantially more difficult than expected (unusual circumstances). However, modifier 22 cannot be used with an Evaluation and Management (E/M) service code. Documentation should detail how the procedure differed from the usual. On the other hand, when services are significantly less than usual, a modifier 25 is used.

If on the day of a procedure there is a need for a physician to provide a separate service because of the patient's condition, then an E/M service may be billed with a 25 modifier. The 25 modifier indicates that the E/M service is significant and separate from the procedure that is performed on the same day by the same physician. When the 25 modifier is used, the documentation for the E/M service should include history, examination, and medical decision making. Even then, carriers may not pay for both the procedure and the visit code.

To recap, modifier 22 is not used with an E/M code and is used to substantiate difficulty of a procedure. Modifier 25 is used with an E/M code that occurs on the same day as a procedure. Use of modifier 25 must be substantiated by documentation.

Modifier 25 should not be confused with modifier 57. Modifier 57 is used to identify the encounter between a patient and a physician during which the initial decision for a major surgery was made. For example, when a patient is seen by a surgeon, and during that visit the decision to perform surgery is made, and the surgery occurs either that day or the next day, the E/M service code must be billed with modifier 57 in order for the surgeon to be paid for the E/M service.

If surgery does not occur either on the day that the decision to perform surgery is made or the next day, there is no need to use modifier 57 with the E/M code. The 57 modifier is used with a visit code to indicate that the decision is made for surgery and that surgery will be done that day or the next.

Modifier 57 is not used with minor surgeries. The decision for minor surgeries is typically done on the spot, and a visit is not billed in addition to the procedure.

Modifier 59 is used to signify a non-E/M service that is independent from another service, such as two different procedures, or separate incisions, lesions, or injury sites.

Modifiers 54 and 55 deal with transfer of operative surgical care. Modifier 54 is applied to the surgical CPT code by the surgeon when the transfer of postoperative care occurs after the surgery (that is, another physician will provide the postoperative care). The other physician then uses modifier 55 for inpatient hospital care and post-discharge. The use of modifiers 54 and 55 requires a written transfer agreement.

Modifier 58 is used for billing staged procedures that have been planned.

When the next step in a surgical procedure occurs, a new postoperative period is set. Modifier 58 is not used when a return to the operating room is required because of complications.

Modifiers 24 and 79 are used during the postoperative period to identify visits and procedures that are unrelated to the surgery. Modifier 24 is used with an E/M code, and modifier 79 is used with a procedure. When modifier 79 is used for a procedure, the postoperative period is reset to the most recent procedure. The physician who used modifier 55 to denote management in the postoperative period will also use modifier 24 when billing for unrelated visits.

Modifier 51 is used to report multiple surgeries. In the case of multiple surgeries, the major surgical procedure should not carry a modifier, but rather modifier 51 should be used to report additional surgical procedures by the same surgeon on the same day.

The following list may be used as a quick-reference guide for when to use the modifiers discussed in this appendix:

- **Modifier 22:** Used when a procedure requires substantially more work (not used with an E/M code)
- **Modifier 24:** Used with an E/M code unrelated to the postoperative period
- **Modifier 25:** Used on the day of the procedure (used with the E/M code to note above and beyond)
- **Modifier 51:** Used for additional procedures performed on the same day after reporting the most major procedure without a modifier
- **Modifier 52:** Used to note that the services provided are less than usual
- **Modifier 54:** Used by the surgeon for surgical care only
- **Modifier 55:** Used by the physician that assumes transfer for postoperative care
- **Modifier 57:** Used with an E/M code (decision for major surgery)
- **Modifier 58:** Used when there is planned staging of procedures (not used for complications)
- **Modifier 59:** Used when there are separate or different procedures (do not use with an E/M code)
- **Modifier 78:** Used when there is a return trip to the operating room for complications
- **Modifier 79:** Used when there is an unrelated procedure during the postoperative period

More in-depth descriptions outlining when modifiers should be used can be found in Appendix A of the CPT codebook.

APPENDIX B

Place of Service Codes

Place of service codes are codes used on providers' claims to identify where a service to the patient was provided. A list of place of service codes can be found in the Current Procedural Terminology (CPT®)* codebook published yearly by the American Medical Association. Codes are given both names and descriptions to ensure appropriate identification. The codes must be available, such as in an organization's administrative system, to ensure correct reporting and payment.

Some places of service are approved for the delivery of some services but not for others. Typically, payers base their place of service policies on the welfare of the insured. Payers want to ensure that a service is delivered in a facility that is equipped adequately to provide the support functions to meet safety standards for the patient.

Place of service codes are reimbursed based on whether the service was provided in a facility or a non-facility as defined in the practice expense portion of the relative value unit scale (RVU PE). A facility (PE-f) is defined as a hospital, skilled nursing facility (SNF), or ambulatory surgery center (ASC). A non-facility (PE-nf) is defined as a physician's office, patient's home, and/or all other facilities, institutions, and care settings except those specifically defined as a facility (PE-f).

Glossary

A

Abuse — Practices that directly or indirectly involve payment for medical services when there is no legal entitlement to that payment. Abuse differs from fraud in that with abuse, the abuser does not knowingly or willingly intend to defraud.

Accounts Receivable — The total amount of money due to a medical practice for services provided.

Accounts Receivable Aging — The total amount of money due to a medical practice categorized by the period of time the money has been due. Typically the categories are: current, > 30 days, > 60 days, > 90 days, > 120 days, > 150 days, and > 180 days.

Adjudication — The process of determining whether a claim will be paid.

Adjustments — The amount of a charge that is written off based on the difference between the fee-for-service charge amount and the contracted amount.

Administrative Simplification Compliance Act — Requires that as of October 16, 2003, providers must submit claims to Medicare electronically to be considered for payment. Exceptions do exist, however, and may be found at www.cms.hhs.gov in Administrative Simplification Compliance Act Self Assessment. (The direct link is: www.cms.hhs.gov/ElectronicBillingEDI-Trans/04_Administrative%20Simplification%20Compliance%20Act%20Enforcement%20Reviews.asp.)

Admission — A patient's entry as an inpatient into a hospital or health care institution.

Advance Beneficiary Notice (ABN) — A written notice given to a Medicare beneficiary before services are provided notifying the beneficiary that the services he or she is about to receive may not be covered by Medicare, and that the beneficiary may be personally responsible for paying for the services identified on the ABN. The patient may decide if he or she wishes to receive those services based on the information provided on the ABN.

Ambulatory Surgery Center (ASC) — A freestanding facility licensed by the Centers for Medicare & Medicaid Services to provide outpatient surgical services. Often referred to as a *same-day surgery center.*

ANSI 837 — The electronic claims format used by both Medicare Part A and Part B providers.

Appeal — A written request asking the insurance carrier to review or critically examine the initial determination of payment for services provided.

Assignment — An agreement to accept as payment in full the allowed amount established by Medicare for services provided. Assignment also refers to the situation when a patient agrees to have payment sent directly to the provider for services provided.

Audits — After a Medicare claim passes the edit process, an audit process checks for duplicate claims and appropriateness of services billed. Medical practices may conduct internal audits in keeping with the organization's compliance plan in order to self-monitor errors in billing for services.

B

Bad Debt — Money in accounts receivable that is owed to the practice but is determined to be uncollectible. The bad debt is written off and removed from accounts receivable.

Balance Billing — A health care organization's attempt to collect from the patient the difference between the standard charge amount and the allowed amount approved by a contracted carrier such as Medicare. Balanced billing is a contract violation and may be illegal. The practice should be avoided.

Beneficiary — An individual who is eligible to receive Medicare or Medicaid benefits to pay for health care services.

Benefit Package — The collection of services an insurance carrier has agreed to pay for under the insurance contract.

Benefit Period — A defined period of time in which the services a Medicare beneficiary uses are measured. A benefit period starts the day a beneficiary goes into a hospital or skilled nursing facility (SNF) and ends when the beneficiary has not received any hospital or SNF care for 60 days. After a benefit period ends, another benefit period begins again when a beneficiary goes into a hospital or SNF. There is no cap on the number of benefit periods for a beneficiary.

Benefit Year — The 12-month period for which the insurance carrier has agreed to pay for services.

Bundling — The inclusion of more than one service into a package to create a global fee for services. Certain services are routinely bundled, and services that have been bundled by the Correct Coding Initiative cannot be unbundled for billing purposes.

C

Capitation — A negotiated monthly payment for a set period of time that is based on the number of members covered under the plan regardless of the charges or amount of services provided to those members during the month.

Carrier — An insurance organization that adjudicates and processes Medicare Part B insurance claims and payments based on a contract with the Centers for Medicare & Medicaid Services.

Carve-Out — Services that are not covered under the normal terms of a contract but are separated out so that special conditions may apply.

Case Management — Coordinated care for a patient who requires extensive services. Case management tries to ensure that the patient receives the appropriate amount of care while reducing the cost of services provided to the patient.

Centers for Medicare & Medicaid Services (CMS) — The federal agency established by Congress as a part of the Department of Health and Human Services to administer and oversee the Medicare program. CMS also is responsible for administering and overseeing portions of Medicaid and other health-related programs. CMS was formerly known as the Health Care Financing Administration (HCFA).

Certificate of Medical Necessity — A form that provides additional information about a claim that supports the provision of certain services.

Charge — The price that is assigned to each unit of service that is delivered to a patient.

Charge Capture — The process of assigning the appropriate charges for all services delivered to the patient so that money can be collected for those services.

Charity Care — Care that is given to patients who do not have the ability to pay for services. The determination for charity care is made before any collection attempt is made.

Claim — A request for payment from an insurance carrier after medical services have been provided.

Clearinghouse — An organization that receives data, in standard or nonstandard format, on behalf of one entity and, after processing the data, sends it to another entity. Clearinghouses include organizations that provide billing, repricing, value-added networks, and community health information systems.

CMS 1500 — The form used to file insurance claims from Medicare Part B providers such as medical offices.

Code Set — A set of codes used to encode data elements of any kind. Code sets established under the Health Insurance Portability and Accountability Act (HIPAA) include both standardized codes and standardized descriptions.

Coinsurance — The percentage of the covered charge that the insured individual is required to pay to satisfy payment for services provided. Coinsurance is paid after insurance pays its portion. The coinsurance percentage amount is established in the benefit plan purchased from the insurance carrier. The insurance deductible must be met before coinsurance is applicable.

Collection Agency — A third-party entity that collects unpaid bills for an organization. Medical practices that are unable to collect payment on accounts from patients may hire a collection agency to collect the debt for medical services. The collection agency receives a contracted percentage of the amount they collect as payment for their services.

Collections — The sum of all medical revenue received as payment for services.

Consolidated Omnibus Budget Reconciliation Act (COBRA) — COBRA provides individuals who lose their health insurance benefits an opportunity to continue insurance coverage for a limited period of time (usually 18 months) by paying 102 percent of the monthly premium to the health plan.

Consultation — An encounter, often including an examination, between a physician and a patient performed at the request of a referring physician to provide advice or opinion about a patient's medical care. The physician who is consulted should document the request for consultation in the patient's chart and should report back in writing to the referring physician all findings and recommendations regarding the request for consultation.

Conversion Factor — A uniform dollar scaling factor that applies relative values to Medicare payments for physicians' services. The conversion factor for the following year is made available March 1 of each year. The intent of the conversion factor is to limit the spending growth rate of the Medicare program.

Coordination of Benefits (COB) — A process for determining and assigning financial responsibility for payment of a claim to prospective payers when two or more insurance payers are providing insurance to the insured individual.

Co-Payment — The required payment amount to be paid by the insured for each medical service as stipulated in the benefit package of the insurance contract. Co-payments are typically paid without regard to coinsurance or deductible.

Correct Coding Initiative (CCI) — Coding regulations intended to prevent fraud and abuse by ensuring that providers are paid correctly for the services provided. CCI is also referred to as the National Correct Coding Initiative (NCCI). Both acronyms are used interchangeably.

Council for Affordable Quality Healthcare (CAQH) —A nonprofit alliance founded by many of the nation's large health plans in cooperation with trade associations to simplify health care administration. One of CAQH's objectives is to provide a Universal Credentialing Data Source for physicians so that they can maintain their credentialing information in a single format. Physicians authorize managed care organizations to access their credentialing information from CAQH. More information may be found by visiting the CAQH Website at www.caqh.org.

Covered Entity — Any health care provider, person, or organization, regardless of size, that provides medical or health services.

Covered Service — An approved medical service that will be paid by insurance.

Credible Coverage — Continuous health coverage of an individual by an employer-sponsored group health plan for 18 months or more.

Current Procedural Terminology (CPT®) — The official standard system of codes established by the American Medical Association for the medical industry. The CPT code set consists of five-digit codes coupled with descriptive terms used to describe each medical service procedure. CPT codes, paired with diagnoses codes (ICD-9), are used to bill for services provided.

D

Date of Service — The date a health care service was provided.

Deductible — The amount an insured individual must pay before insurance begins to pay for covered services. Deductibles are met at the beginning of each plan year and are defined by the insurance contract.

Department of Health and Human Services (HHS) — The U.S. federal agency that administers health and welfare programs. HHS is the parent agency of the Centers for Medicare & Medicaid Services.

Diagnosis — The identification of a patient's medical condition or disease and is represented for billing purposes by an International Classification of Diseases, Ninth Revision (ICD-9) code.

Diagnosis-Related Groups (DRGs) — A classification system of 383 major diagnosis categories based on the International Classification of Diseases, Ninth Revision (ICD-9) codes.

Direct Contracting — A method of bypassing insurance carriers in which employers or businesses contract directly with health care providers for specified services. Direct contracting is usually done following Employee Retirement Income Security Act (ERISA) guidelines.

Disabled Insured — Refers to disabled persons who are entitled to disability benefits from Social Security or the Railroad Retirement Board (RRB). After 24 months of disability, individuals are automatically entitled to Medicare Part A.

Discounted Fee-For-Service — A negotiated rate for services that is less than the full fee-for-service rate and is accepted as payment in full.

Disenrollment — A process of deleting insurance coverage to individuals or groups.

Documentation — The record of medical services provided to satisfy documentation guidelines.

Duplicate Claims — Medicare considers the act of billing for the same service more than one time as filing duplicate claims. Medicare condemns this practice when repeated regularly.

Durable Medical Equipment (DME) — Reusable medical equipment ordered by a provider for a patient's home use.

Durable Power of Attorney — A legal document providing for the appointment of an agent to act on behalf of an individual in financial and health care matters if the individual becomes mentally incapacitated.

E

Edits — The process used to verify that the information on a claim is complete and valid.

Electronic Data Interchange (EDI) — The process of using the American National Standards Institute (ANSI) Accredited Standards Committee (ASC) x12 format to exchange data between organizations via electronic transmission. As a provision of the Health Insurance Portability and Accountability Act (HIPAA), EDI ensures that private health information and data will be protected. EDI enrollment requires providers to declare which parties are authorized to submit or receive transactions on behalf of the provider. When a provider makes changes to that authority, that information must also be communicated.

Electronic Funds Transfer (EFT) — Electronic transmission of a provider's payment for services sent directly to the financial institution selected by the provider.

Electronic Medical Record (EMR) — A computerized medical records program used to capture and retain the medical record of patients as a replacement for a paper chart.

Electronic Remittance Advise (ERA) — An electronically transmitted explanation of benefits for payment of health insurance claims sent to providers.

Eligibility Date — The first date an individual can access covered health insurance benefits.

Eligible — Refers to individuals qualified to receive benefits as defined by a specific health plan.

Emergency — A medical situation that is severe or life-threatening and requires immediate medical intervention. In emergency situations, health plans allow for pre-certification/pre-authorization after treatment (the time period is defined by the health plan).

Employee Retirement Income Security Act (ERISA) — A federal act governing pension and benefit plans that includes regulations regarding health care plans for employees. ERISA covers health care benefit plan design and prohibits discrimination.

Employer Identification Number (EIN) — The Internal Revenue Service's tax identifying number used in all standard transactions.

Encounter — A face-to-face contact between a patient and a provider during which medical services are provided and the provider documents those services.

End Stage Renal Disease (ESRD) Insured — Refers to individuals receiving dialysis treatments or a kidney transplant who have met the eligibility conditions to qualify for Medicare Part A.

Enrollment — Refers to the time when an eligible person establishes membership in a health plan.

Evaluation and Management (E/M) Codes — A set of CPT codes used to define graduated levels of face-to-face medical services provided to a patient by a provider. The levels of service are based on the number of elements performed by the provider and the intensity of medical involvement in three areas: (1) medical history, (2) physical examination, and (3) medical decision making.

Evergreen Contract — A contract between a provider and payer that renews automatically, if not specifically cancelled, after the initial term of the contract.

Exclusion or Excluded Services — Any services that will not be covered by a health plan.

Exclusion List — A list provided by the Office of the Investigator General (OIG) that identifies sanctioned providers who are excluded from Medicare reimbursement.

Explanation of Benefits (EOB) — A written description of payment made by a health plan that is sent to both provider and patient.

F

Facility (PE-f) — As a part of the practice expense portion of the relative value unit scale (RVU PE), a facility (PE-f) refers to hospital, skilled nursing facility (SNF), or ambulatory surgery center (ASC). A non-facility (PE-nf) refers to a physician's office, patient's home, or any other care facility/institution that is not designated as a facility (PE-f).

False Claims Act — Legislation that prohibits filing insurance claims that are known to be false, fictitious, or fraudulent.

Federal Employees Health Benefits Program (FEHB) — The largest employer-sponsored health insurance program covering employees of the federal government.

Fee-For-Service — Charges for medical services based on the standard fee schedule of the practice with the expectation that fees will be paid as charged.

Fee Schedule — A complete list of Current Procedural Terminology (CPT) codes and corresponding fees that are based on the services provided by a practice. Each payer may have a different fee schedule that dictates reimbursement for the medical practice, and each payer may pay a different amount per CPT code based on contract negotiations.

Fiscal Intermediary — A contractor hired by the Centers for Medicare & Medicaid Services to process claims. Since 2006 a fiscal intermediary is now referred to as a medicare administrative contractor (MAC).

Fraud — Knowingly, willingly, and intentionally deceiving or misrepresenting the truth, knowing that such actions will result in an unauthorized benefit either directly or indirectly.

Fraud and Abuse — A common term used broadly to refer to intentional deception (fraud) and reckless conduct (abuse) in the health care arena. The distinction between fraud and abuse is based on specific facts relating to intent and prior knowledge.

G

Gatekeeper — In a managed care arena, a primary care physician who manages a patient's care and makes referrals when necessary.

Global Billing — Invoicing for both the technical and professional components of diagnostic testing. Global billing is used when the same physician performs a diagnostic test and interprets the results.

Global Period — Refers to the amount of time needed to complete all normal services related to a surgery including pre- and postoperative care in a single payment. Preoperative care is one day prior to the surgery. Postoperative care varies based on the intensity of the surgery. Major surgeries have 90-day postoperative periods and minor surgeries have either 0 or 10 days.

Global Surgical Package — Refers to the usual pre- and postoperative care pertaining to a particular Current Procedural Terminology (CPT) code for a surgical procedure.

Gross Charges — The total charges for services before any discounts or adjustments are made.

Group Health Plan — A health insurance contract purchased from a health insurance carrier by an employer to provide health insurance coverage to employees.

Guarantee Issue — Refers to the guarantee by the Health Insurance Portability and Accountability Act (HIPAA) that individuals who have lost insurance coverage by an employee-sponsored group health plan, for reasons other than nonpayment of premiums, cannot be denied the opportunity to purchase health care insurance if they have exhausted all Consolidated Omnibus Budget Reconciliation Act (COBRA) coverage, even if they have a pre-existing medical condition.

H

Healthcare Common Procedure Coding System (HCPCS) — A standardized coding system based on the American Medical Association's Current Procedural Terminology (CPT) code set that is intended to ensure that health insurance claims are processed in a consistent and orderly manner. HCPCS is divided into two major subsystems. HCPCS Level I includes the CPT codes that describe procedures and services. HCPCS Level II identifies products, supplies, and services that are not defined by CPT codes. HCPCS Level II codes are referred to as *alphanumeric codes* — a single alpha plus four numeric digits. Examples of the services not covered by CPT codes that are billed by Level II codes are ambulance services and durable medical equipment. CMS maintains the HCPCS Level II code set.

Health Insurance Portability and Accountability Act of 1996 (HIPAA) — HIPAA legislation was passed by Congress to (1) establish health care standards in several areas, (2) provide health insurance portability to individuals changing jobs, and (3) reduce fraud and abuse. The Administrative Simplification provision of HIPAA defines standards for transaction requirements including the adoption of code sets, identifiers, privacy, and security. Individuals who can prove continuous health insurance coverage cannot be denied benefits for preexisting conditions when moving to another health plan for coverage.

Health Maintenance Organization (HMO) — A managed care insurance organization providing a broad range of defined coverage to an enrolled population. Services are contracted through a certain panel of providers at discounted rates.

Health Plan — An insurance entity that provides coverage for contracted individuals and groups to cover all or a portion of payment for health care services. These payers may be group health plans, indemnity insurance companies, health maintenance organizations, or government assistance plans such as Medicare, Medicaid, TRICARE, and Indian Health Services.

Health Reimbursement Account (HRA) — A type of insurance program in which an employer partially reimburses participating employees for the cost of health services. An HRA is partially self-funded by the employer who pays a premium, up to a cap, and receives business expense tax savings when distributions are made. After the cap has been reached, the traditional policy kicks in. HRAs look like traditional insurance to the insured and are largely designed at the discretion of the employer. The insured typically pays physician co-payments, drug card co-payments, deductibles, and coinsurance. HRAs differ from Health Savings Accounts (HSAs) in that no separate savings account is set up.

Health Savings Account (HSA) — A medical savings account that allows both individuals and employers with high-deductible insurance policies to contribute tax free to an account for paying current or future qualified medical expenses. Provided for by the Medicare Prescription Drug, Improvement and Modernization Act of 2003, HSAs are portable and place spending responsibility on the individual.

Hospital Encounter — A direct encounter between a patient and provider in a hospital setting. Like ambulatory/office encounters, these encounters require a documented face-to-face contact between patient and provider. These visits are billed using Evaluation and Management (E/M) codes.

Hospitalist — A physician who works in a hospital who facilitates hospital admissions and fulfills a primary care function for the patient. A hospitalist, as the physician of record for patients in the hospital, manages their patients' care across specialties.

I

Incident to Services — Necessary medical services provided to a patient by a practitioner who is under the direct supervision of a physician who is in the office suite at the time the service is provided and with whom the practitioner has a collaborative agreement.

Indemnity Insurance — A type of fee-for-service insurance plan. Indemnity health care insurance differs from health maintenance organizations and preferred provider organizations in that it allows the insured more choice in selecting providers. The insured receives health care services that are billed to the carrier, who pays a percentage of the billed charges, with the balance of the charge paid by the insured.

Independence Practice Association/Organization (IPA/IPO) — An organization that negotiates and secures insurance contracts for a block of physician members with health plans. Physicians may belong to an IPA/IPO, which is a legal entity, separate and apart from the legal entity structure of their medical practice.

Inquiry — A written request for claims information.

Insurance Company — An organization that creates health plans for purchase by groups and/or individuals that will indemnify members and guarantee to pay certain portions of health care services if insurance premiums are paid in keeping with the terms of the insurance contract.

International Classification of Diseases, Ninth Revision (ICD-9) — An international coding system for diagnoses that was developed and maintained by the World Health Organization to track diagnoses worldwide. For billing and reimbursement purposes, ICD-9 diagnosis codes are paired with Current Procedural Terminology (CPT) procedural codes based on services provided.

J

J-Codes —A subset of the Healthcare Common Procedure Coding System (HCPCS) Level II codes that are used to identify certain drugs.

Joint Commission —The accreditation body for hospitals and other health care institutions. Formerly known as the Joint Commission on Accreditation of Healthcare Organizations (JCAHO), the Joint Commission conducts surveys to ensure compliance with accreditation standards such as patient safety.

K

Kickback — Compensation or other reward for services or favors received often because of confidential agreement. Offering, requesting, or receiving remuneration for referrals of Medicare or Medicaid patients is prohibited.

L

Lifetime Limit — The collective amount an insurance carrier will pay out for health care services over the insured's lifetime. This amount goes beyond a current insurance year.

Local Coverage Policy — Medicare contractors are free to determine local coverage policy when there are not any national coverage policies in place.

Local Coverage Policy/ Local Coverage Determinations (LCD) — Medicare contractors are free to determine, in conjunction with their clinicians, local coverage policy when there are not any national coverage policies in place. LCDs specify what services are reasonable and necessary and under what circumstances. LCDs are intended to serve as educational and administrative tools to help providers understand how to submit claims correctly to be paid. The other type of coverage policy is National Coverage Determinations (NCDs).

M

Managed Care — Discounted medical insurance for employers providing health care insurance coverage to their employees. Managed care plans focus on controlling cost by reducing utilization and treatment. Managed care plans vary greatly in benefits provided and out-of-pocket expenses. Types of managed care plans are health maintenance organizations (HMOs), preferred provider organizations (PPOs), and point-of-service (POS) plans.

Maximum Allowable Charge — The highest amount a provider can charge for a particular service. The maximum allowable charge is set by the insurance carrier.

Medicaid — A federal health care program that is administered by the states with state-specific benefit and coverage guidelines. Medicaid, established by

Title 19, an amendment of the Social Security Act, is intended to provide health care services to certain groups, primarily the indigent. The Medicaid program for each state is partially funded by the federal government.

Medical Group Practice — A group of three or more physicians legally affiliated to provide health care services.

Medical Necessity — Services and supplies that align with the accepted standard of care for a particular medical diagnosis meet the criteria for medical necessity.

Medical Power of Attorney — A legal document that allows an individual to appoint an agent to make decisions regarding that individual's medical treatment, including the right to agree to, refuse, or withdraw treatment. Health personnel must respect the agent's designated authority and inform the agent of all information regarding treatment options. A medical power of attorney differs from a living will in that its provisions are broader than life-sustaining procedures.

Medical Record — The complete set of documentation relating to the care of a patient within an organization. A paper record is also known as a *chart* while an electronic record is known as an *EMR* (electronic medical record).

Medical Review — A review of billing practices that is conducted when billing patterns that are atypical or problematic are identified.

Medicare — A federal health program with oversight by the Centers for Medicare & Medicaid Services. Medicare, established by Title 18, an amendment of the Social Security Act, is intended to provide health care services to the elderly, younger people with disabilities, and patients with end stage renal disease (ESRD). Medicare is funded by the federal government and in part by payroll taxes paid by both employers and employees.

Medicare Administrative Contractor (MAC) — A third-party organization that contracts with the Centers for Medicare & Medicaid Services to administer the Medicare program. These contractors, formerly know as Fiscal Intermediaries for Medicare Part A and Carriers for Medicare Part B, were combined under a single authority known as MACs in 2006.

Medicare Parts A, B, C, and D — The four subcategories of Medicare that govern different aspects of coverage. Part A covers inpatient hospital care, skilled nursing facilities, hospice, and some home health care. Part B covers physicians' and outpatient services. Part C covers Medicare Advantage managed care plans for Medicare beneficiaries eligible for Part A and enrolled in Part B. Part D is a stand-alone prescription drug plan chosen by beneficiaries.

Medicare Physician Fee Schedule (MPFS) — Medicare's yearly, Part B, reimbursement schedule for physicians' services. MPFS uses Resource-Based Relative Value Scale (RBRVS) components — work, practice, and malpractice expenses — to calculate fees.

Medicare Remittance Advice (RA) — The information sent to providers from Medicare contractors to explain and justify reimbursement decisions.

Medicare Summary Notice (MSN) — A notice received by beneficiaries every 90 days listing all services billed to Medicare, the amounts paid, and the amount that the beneficiary is responsible to pay.

Medigap — A supplemental insurance policy for Medicare beneficiaries designed to fill in the payment gaps of Medicare health benefits coverage. Medigap policies are sold by private insurance carriers and typically cover co-insurance payment of Medicare, but each plan has a different set of benefits. Physician practices are required to file Medicare claims for beneficiaries, and Medicare is required to "crossover" or send on Medigap claims for secondary payment. Crossover occurs after a beneficiary has signed authorization for reassignment of Medigap benefits.

Modifiers — Numeric codes that increase or decrease the relative value unit (RVU) of a Current Procedural Terminology (CPT) code. A complete list of modifiers with definitions is found in the CPT codebook.

Multi-Specialty Practice — Refers to a group of physicians who practice different specialties working together in a medical group that is a legal entity.

Multi-Tiered Plan — An insurance plan designed to offer coverage choices to plan members. Choices are priced based on benefits such as networks and coinsurance.

N

National Correct Coding Initiative (NCCI) — Coding regulations intended to prevent fraud and abuse by ensuring that providers are paid correctly for the services provided. NCCI is also referred to as the Correct Coding Initiative. Both acronyms are used interchangeably.

National Coverage Determinations (NCDs) — NCDs are Medicare regulations determined by statutory and policy framework and applied on a national basis for all Medicare beneficiaries. NCDs are categorized by medical procedures, supplies, and diagnostic services. The other type of coverage policy is Local Coverage Determinations (LCDs).

National Payer Identifier — A system to uniquely identify health plans.

National Provider Identifier (NPI) — A system used by health plans that uniquely identifies providers of health care services. The NPI replaces the unique physician identifier number (UPIN) and is mandated by the Health Insurance Portability and Accountability Act (HIPAA).

Network — The group of health care providers with whom a health plan has contracted so that its insured can access health care services at discounted rates.

Non-Assigned Claim — A Medicare claim filed by a non-participating provider. The patient, as beneficiary, will directly receive the reimbursement for the services provided.

Non-Facility (PE-nf) — As a part of the practice expense portion of the relative value unit scale (RVU PE), a non-facility (PE-nf) refers to a physician's office, patient's home, or any other care facility/institution that is not designated as a facility (PE-f). A facility refers to a hospital, skilled nursing facility, or ambulatory surgery center.

Non-Participating Physician — A physician who does not participate with a health plan and does not agree to abide by the health plan's terms for payment. A non-participating provider may collect the difference between the amount insurance pays and the provider's standard charge for the service.

Non-Physician Provider — Refers to licensed providers of health care services, which include audiologists, Certified Registered Nurse Anesthetists (CRNAs), midwives, nurse practitioners, occupational therapists, optometrists, physical therapists, physician assistants, psychologists, social workers, and surgeon's assistants.

Notice of Exclusions of Medicare Benefits — A notice from Medicare that advises a beneficiary in advance of receiving services that Medicare will not pay.

O

Office of Inspector General (OIG) — A division of the Department of Health and Human Services that protects the integrity of the Medicare and Medicaid programs by conducting audits, investigations, inspections, and other functions that may identify noncompliance.

Offset — When a provider has received a second payment that is duplicative, an offset is required to collect or recover by recoup the duplicate payment.

Open Access — Refers to a health plan's policy allowing its insured members to access the services of a specialist without a primary care referral.

Open Enrollment Period — A specified period of time designated to enroll in a health plan.

Out-of-Network —Refers to services provided by a physician with whom the insurance carrier does not have a negotiated contract. The insured can expect those services to cost more than services provided by a network provider.

Out-of-Pocket Maximum — The maximum amount the insured will have to pay personally. The out-of-pocket amount is dictated by the health plan's benefits package. Once health care services expenses have reached this amount, insurance pays 100 percent of future expenses during the current health care contract.

Overpayment — Payment in excess of what is due. When a claim adjustment creates an overpayment to a provider, an account receivable from that provider is created and a demand letter for repayment is sent to the provider. If the provider does not send payment for the amount, the amount will subsequently be recouped from the provider's future payments.

P

Participating Provider — A medical services provider who has voluntarily agreed to accept assignment on all claims benefits considered a covered service for Medicare beneficiaries.

Payer — One who pays for health care services.

Payer Mix — Payers are divided by category such Medicare, Medicaid, managed care, discounted fee-for-service, and self-pay. The payer mix is the percentage of each category based on the total patient population.

Pay for Performance (P4P) — A health care payment incentive system based on quality outcomes and other measures.

Physician — A qualified and licensed doctor of medicine (MD) or a doctor of osteopathy (DO) who provides medical care to patients.

Place of Service Codes — Codes used on providers' claims to identify where a service to the patient was provided.

Point of Service (POS) — A type of health care plan that incorporates features from both fee-for-service and health maintenance organization plans. POS plans require a gatekeeper primary care physician to see a patient and to provide a referral before the patient sees a specialist while allowing the insured to get services from other providers at additional cost.

Portability — As provided by the Health Insurance Portability and Accountability Act (HIPAA), individuals may change to a new insurance plan with continuous coverage provided they have had prior continuous credible coverage for 18 months.

Pre-Certification — Contact with a payer prior to providing a medical service to its insured that allows a payer the ability to assess whether the planned medical treatment is appropriate treatment for the insured's medical condition. Pre-certification is no guarantee that medical services will be paid by the payer. Pre-certification is also called *prior authorization*.

Pre-Existing Condition — A medical condition that a patient had before the patient was covered by his or her current insurance plan. Assuming that the insured had not had credible coverage for the previous 18 months as dictated by the Health Insurance Portability and Accountability Act (HIPAA), the carrier may not cover that condition until after a period of time, which is usually 12 months.

Preferred Provider Organization (PPO) — A type of health care plan in which a group of providers contract with an organization at discounted rates to provide medical services. PPOs are managed care plans similar to health maintenance organizations but allow employees to choose to see a provider either in the plan or outside of the plan. Seeing a provider who is not a plan member will cost the patient more than seeing a provider who is a plan member.

Pricer/Repricer — The health care insurance plan employee who exercises the act of determining the eligibility and the actual covered amount of the service based on the plan's quoted benefits for billed services.

Primary Care Physician (PCP) — A provider who offers a broad range of basic medical services in practices, such as family practice, internal medicine, pediatrics, and geriatrics, and who can offer those services over an extended period of time in the patient's life span. A PCP is designated as a gatekeeper in a managed care plan.

Prior Authorization — An insurance requirement to review and approve the expected delivery of medical services before services are provided to ensure that services are necessary and appropriate. Prior authorization, also called *pre-certification*, is used as an attempt to reduce utilization and control the health plan's cost.

Professional Component (PC) — One of the two components of a diagnostic test — the professional component (PC) and the technical component (TC) — that represents the physician evaluating the test results. If the PC is billed for separate reimbursement, it is represented by attaching Modifier 26 to the Current Procedural Terminology (CPT) code.

Professional Courtesy — The act of forgiving or discounting the cost of medical services to certain people. Professional courtesy has been a long-standing tradition; however, under the Health Insurance Portability and Accountability Act (HIPAA), this practice is addressed in the anti-kickback amendments where remuneration is defined, in part, as waving all or part of coinsurance or deductibles. Although the law does allow an exception for financial need, traditionally, professional courtesy has been the determination to "accept insurance only" as payment in full. (*Note:* This policy is not in keeping with Medicare program regulations.) Any link between professional courtesy provided and subsequent referrals of Medicare or Medicaid patients could put a provider in a vulnerable position to be prosecuted on a fraud and abuse case or in violation of anti-kickback statutes. In the case of non-government insurance carriers, providers should depend on the requirements of their agreements with the insurance carrier to dictate their policy toward professional courtesy.

Protected Health Information (PHI) — Refers to the personal and identifiable health information a covered entity must protect. PHI held or transmitted in any form whether electronic, paper, or oral is protected under the Health Insurance Portability and Accountability Act (HIPAA).

Providers — Licensed individuals and institutions that provide health care services.

R

Re-Aged Accounts Receivable — Refers to an account balance that is reset to 0 days in accounts receivable because of payment activity.

Record Retention — The amount of time health care services records should be kept on file by a health care organization. Organizations should check with their Certified Public Accountant to receive a definition of the period of time records should be retained. Time frames will vary based on the type of information contained in the record, such as whether the information is organizational financial information or patient health treatment information.

Recoupment — The act of holding back money from payments due to a provider as a method of recovering prior overpayments.

Relative Value Unit (RVU) — A standardized collective value assigned to a procedure or service for reimbursement purposes. An RVU is part of the Resource-Based Relative Value Scale (RBRVS) payment schedule and considers work value, practice expense, and medical liability expense as well as whether the service is provided in a facility or non-facility.

Remittance Advise — The summary of payments and adjustments sent to a provider containing information relating to one or more insured.

Resource-Based Relative Value Scale (RBRVS) — A standardized physician payment schedule in which values are assigned to Current Procedural Terminology (CPT) codes that the Centers for Medicare & Medicaid uses to determine Medicare reimbursement.

S

Self-Insurance — A form of health care coverage in which an organization assumes the financial risk of health care coverage for its employees instead of purchasing insurance.

Self-Pay — Refers to the act of paying a medical practice directly for services provided. Patients who self-pay do not use insurance.

Social Security Act — The public law enacted in 1935 whose amendments provide for Medicare and Medicaid.

Subscriber — A group such as an employer or union that contracts on behalf of its members for health care services.

T

Technical Component (TC) — One of the two components of a diagnostic test — the professional component (PC) and the technical component (TC) — that represents the labor cost of the test. When the physician performs both portions of a diagnostic test (he or she performs the test and evaluates the results), the test is billed as a global fee. The TC and the PC together make up the global fee.

Third-Party Administrator (TPA) — An organization contracted by health plans to process insurance claims. TPAs provide administrative services such as collecting premiums and adjudicating and paying claims for the health plan's insured members.

Third-Party Payer — The organization that pays providers for the health care services used by enrollees in their health care plans.

Timely Filing — The concept of requiring that claims be filed within a certain period of time from the date the service was provided in order to be considered for payment. Providers of health care services have a specified length of time from the date that the service was provided to file a health insurance claim. Medicare has a rolling time limit that depends on the month in which the service was provided. Commercial carriers vary in timely filing specifications, usually ranging from 9 to 18 months.

TRICARE — The health plan for active duty and retired members of the Department of Defense's uniformed services. TRICARE was formerly known as the Civilian Health and Medical Program of the Uniformed Services (CHAMPUS).

U

Unbundling — The billing term used to describe billing separately for elements of a service that are intended to be billed as a single fee.

Underpayment — The term used when Medicare erroneously cuts the payment amount on an insurance claim. Medicare is required to correct the error without action on the part of the provider.

Unprocessable Claim — A claim that cannot be processed due to incorrect or incomplete information.

Usual, Customary, and Reasonable (UCR) — Refers to the typical charge for a particular medical service area. Using UCR, some carriers may try to negotiate a one-time payment rate on a specific claim when the provider is a non-participating provider.

Utilization — Refers to the frequency of which health care services are used.

Utilization Review — The process of evaluating a provider to ensure that the services ordered meet medical necessity requirements.

V

Vendor — A third-party seller of goods and/or services.

W

Whistle-Blower — A person who knows of wrongdoing, fraud, or abuse by a provider and reports that information to the federal government or wronged party so that legal action can be brought against the wrongdoer.

Workers' Compensation — Mandated coverage that employers must provide for their employees to cover work-related injuries. The employer must be aware of and approve of the employee seeking services (i.e., the employer must agree that the injury was work related and communicate to the workers' compensation carrier) before workers' compensation insurance will pay for services provided.

X

X12 837 — The term used to refer to the Health Insurance Portability and Accountability Act (HIPAA) national transactions standards for submitting electronic claims to Medicare and for coordinating benefits with other payer trading partners. Version 4010A1 was the implementation guide adopted as the national standard. Other guide versions, such as ASC X12 5051, may offer updates.

About the Author

Sarah J. Holt, PhD, FACMPE, is the administrator of several health care organizations in Cape Girardeau, Missouri. Sarah provides practice management for Cape Girardeau Surgical Clinic, Inc. & Breast Care Center and for The Breast Care & Diagnostic Center as well as Cape Medical Billing Corp, a medical practice billing company. Additionally, she is the administrator of Cape Girardeau Doctors' Park, which offers a full range of medical services on an 80-acre complex comprised of 35 medical buildings.

Sarah received a PhD in Policy Analysis with a health care emphasis from St. Louis University, a master's in counseling from Southeast Missouri State University, and an undergraduate degree in education. She has done extensive research on how medical office insurance staff members make decisions relating to insurance reimbursement and how complexity influences organizations. She teaches health policy and health care reimbursement at the graduate level at Southeast Missouri State University and speaks on health care management topics to audiences of physicians, management, and staff.

Sarah's leadership has led Cape Girardeau Surgical Clinic, Inc., to be recognized as a Medical Group Management Association (MGMA) Better Performer numerous times. For many years Sarah has been an active participant of the American College of Medical Practice Executives (ACMPE) and in MGMA at local, state, and national levels. She is a Fellow in the American College of Medical Practice Executives and a past chair of the ACMPE Board of Directors.

Index

A

ABN (Advance Beneficiary Notice),
  109–10
Abuse
  defined, 78, 109, 116
  in documentation process, 77–78
Accounts receivable
  account follow-up, 82–85
  claim appeal process, 84–85
  defined, 109
  prioritizing work, 82–83
  re-aged, 124
  rejections and denials, 83–84
Accounts receivable aging, 109
Adjudication, 109
Adjustments, 109
Administrative law judge (ALJ), 84–85
Administrative Simplification Compli-
  ance Act (2003), 109
Admission, 109
Advance Beneficiary Notice (ABN), 6,
  109–10
Advantage plans, 3, 6, 8
AFDC (Aid to Families with Dependent
  Children), 9
Aid to Families with Dependent Chil-
  dren (AFDC), 9
ALJ (administrative law judge), 84–85
Allowable amount, 14
Ambulatory surgery center. *See* ASC (am-
  bulatory surgery center)
American Hospital Association, 20
American Medical Association

Relative Value Scale Update Commit-
  tee, 48
standard system of codes, 45–46, 107,
  113
ANSI (American National Standards
  Institute), 114
ANSI 837 format, 110
Appeals, 84–85, 110
ASC (ambulatory surgery center)
  defined, 110
  as facility, 115
  place of service codes, 107
Assignment, 110
Audits, 110

B

Bad debt, 110
Balance billing, 110
Balanced Budget Act (1997), 3
BCBS (Blue Cross Blue Shield), 19–20
Beneficiaries, 7–8, 110
Benefit package, 110
Benefit period, 110
Benefit year, 110
Billing process
  CCI and, 48–52
  claims format, 59–60
  CPT and, 45–46
  E/M examinations and, 76
  global surgical packages, 103–4
  goal of, 45
  ICD-9 coding, 46–47
  insurance verification, 54–57

Medicare Claims Processing Manual, 59
OIG compliance guidelines and, 58–59
patient paperwork, 52–54
role of HIPAA, 57–58
RVUs and, 47–48
Blue Cross Blue Shield (BCBS), 19–20
BN (budget neutrality), 48
BNA (budget neutrality adjustment), 48
BNDD (Bureau of Narcotics and Danger-
ous Drugs), 72
Budget neutrality (BN), 48
Budget neutrality adjustment (BNA), 48
Bundling services, 111
Bureau of Narcotics and Dangerous
Drugs (BNDD), 72

C

Capitation, 111
CAQH (Council for Affordable Quality
Healthcare), 74, 113
Carriers. *See* Insurance carriers
Carve-out, 111
Case management, 111
CC (Chief Complaint), 75
CCI (Correct Coding Initiative)
billing process and, 48–52
bundling services, 111
defined, 7, 48–49, 112
edits table, 49–52
*National Correct Coding Initiative Cod-
ing Policy Manual for Medicare
Services*, 49
scenario, 89–90
Centers for Medicare & Medicaid Services.
See CMS (Centers for Medicare &
Medicaid Services)
Certificate of Medical Necessity, 111
Certified nurse midwife (CNM), 45
CF (conversion factor), 47–48, 112
CHAMPUS. *See* TRICARE
Charge, 111, 126
Charge capture
defined, 65–66, 111
scenario, 98–100
Charge entry, 66
Chief Complaint (CC), 75
Claims
accuracy of, 80–81
appeal process, 84–85
defined, 111
filing, 78–81, 91
format considerations, 59–60, 66–67
fraud and abuse, 77–78
generating, 66–67

information overload, 26–27
Medicare Claims Processing Manual, 59
Medicare processing of, 3–4
non-assigned, 5, 121
rejections and denials, 83–84
reopening, 85
scenario, 93–94
submitting, 66–67
timely filing, 126
unprocessable, 126
working, 67–68
Clearinghouses, 78–79, 111
Clinical nurse specialist (CNS), 45
CME (continuing medical education), 74
CMS (Centers for Medicare & Medicaid
Services)
claims format, 59–60
coding requirements, 74–75
confusing regulations, 45
defined, 111
documentation requirements, 74–75
GA modifiers, 6
HHS and, 113
Medicare claims processing, 3
Medicare Part D and, 3
MIP and, 77
MPFS updates, 48
MUE program, 51–52
RBRVS system, 47
Standard EDI Enrollment Form, 60
CMS 1500 form, 54, 112
CMS-20033 form, 85
CMS-20034 A/B form, 85
CNM (certified nurse midwife), 45
CNS (clinical nurse specialist), 45
COB (coordination of benefits)
claims format, 59
defined, 112
Medicare provided, 56
COBRA (Consolidated Omnibus Budget
Reconciliation Act)
defined, 17–18, 112
guarantee issue, 117
as primary payer, 7, 56
Code sets, 60, 112
Coding services, 74–75, 94
Coinsurance
defined, 14–15, 112
fee-for-service plans and, 5
Collection agency, 87, 112
Collections
credit balances, 87–88
defined, 112
offsets, 88

in revenue cycle, 87–88
Commercial for-profit insurance
    about, 11–12
    direct contracting, 18–19, 113
    discounted fee-for-service, 12, 114
    fee-for-service plans, 12–13, 116
    managed care plans, 12–18, 119
    worker's compensation, 18, 126–27
Consolidated Omnibus Budget Recon-
        ciliation Act. See COBRA (Consoli-
        dated Omnibus Budget Reconcili-
        ation Act)
Consultation, 112
Continuing medical education (CME), 74
Contracting, 63–64
Conversion factor (CF), 47–48, 112
Coordination of benefits (COB)
    claims format, 59
    defined, 112
    Medicare provided, 56
Co-payment, 13–14, 112
Correct Coding Initiative. See CCI (Cor-
        rect Coding Initiative)
Correspondence
    with insurance carriers, 86
    with patients, 86–87
    in revenue cycle, 86–87
Council for Affordable Quality Health-
        care (CAQH), 74, 113
Covered entity, 57, 113
Covered services, 113
CPT (Current Procedural Terminology)
    defined, 45–46, 113
    documentation requirements, 74–75
    E/M codes, 115
    GA modifier, 6
    global surgical package, 103, 116
    HCPCS and, 117
    HIPAA regulations, 60
    ICD-9 codes and, 118
    modifiers, 103–5
    place of service codes, 107
    on professional component, 124
    RVUs and, 121
    scenario, 99
Credentialing, physician, 70–74
Credible coverage, 113
Current Procedural Terminology. See CPT
        (Current Procedural Terminology)

D

Date of service, 113
DEA (Drug Enforcement Administra-
        tion), 73

Decision making
    as influence in Medicare implementa-
        tion, 40–41
    medical, 76
Deductible
    defined, 14, 113
    managed care plans, 13
    Medicare Part A, 6
Department of Health and Human
        Services. See HHS (Department of
        Health and Human Services)
Diagnoses
    code sets on, 60
    defined, 113
    medical decision making, 76
Diagnosis-Related Groups (DRGs), 113
Direct contracting, 18–19, 113
Disabled insured
    defined, 113
    Medicare and, 56
    scenario, 96
Discounted fee-for-service, 12, 114
Disenrollment, 114
DME (durable medical equipment), 114
Documentation
    adhering to regulations, 24–26
    CMS requirements, 74–75
    defined, 114
    fraud and abuse, 77–78
    OIG compliance guidelines and, 59
DRGs (Diagnosis-Related Groups), 113
Drug Enforcement Administration
        (DEA), 73
Duplicate claims, 114
Durable medical equipment (DME), 114
Durable power of attorney, 114

E

EDI (electronic data interchange),
        59–60, 114
Edits, 114
EFT (electronic funds transfer)
    defined, 114
    HIPAA regulation, 60
    payment posting, 81
EIN (Employer Identification Number),
        115
Electronic claims
    ANSI 837 format, 110
    format considerations, 59, 66–67
    generating, 66–67
    payment posting, 81
    submitting, 66–67
    X12 837 standard, 127

Electronic data interchange (EDI), 59–60, 114
Electronic funds transfer (EFT)
  defined, 114
  HIPAA regulation, 60
  payment posting, 81
Electronic medical record (EMR), 114
Electronic remittance advice (ERA), 114
Eligibility data, 114
Eligible
  defined, 114
  Medicaid considerations, 9
  Medical coverage considerations, 4
E/M (Evaluation and Management)
  code sets on, 60
  CPT codes, 45–46
  defined, 115
  documentation requirements, 75–76
  hospital encounter, 118
  modifiers, 104–5
  OIG compliance guidelines, 59
  RBRVS system, 47
  scenario, 94–95
  timely filing, 79–80
Emergency, 114–15
Employee Retirement Income Security Act (ERISA), 113, 115
Employer Identification Number (EIN), 115
EMR (electronic medical record), 114
Encounter, 115
End stage renal disease. *See* ESRD (end stage renal disease)
EOB (explanation of benefits)
  defined, 115
  interpreting, 23–24, 67–69
  non-participation, 70
  participation, 69–70
  reading, 68–69
  scenario, 90–91, 98–99
  working claims, 67–68
ERA (electronic remittance advice), 114
ERISA (Employee Retirement Income Security Act), 113, 115
ESRD (end stage renal disease)
  defined, 115
  Medicare and, 2, 7, 56, 120
Evaluation and Management. *See* E/M (Evaluation and Management)
Evergreen contract, 115
Exclusion list, 115
Exclusion/excluded services, 115
Explanation of benefits. *See* EOB (explanation of benefits)

F

Facility (PE-f), 107, 115
False Claims Act, 115
Federal Black Lung Program, 7, 56
Federal Employees Health Benefits Program. *See* FEHB (Federal Employees Health Benefits Program)
Federal government. *See also* Rules and regulations
  government insurance, 1–2
  Medicaid, 8–10, 119–20
  Medicare, 2–8, 120
  Medicare claims processing, 3
  physician credentialing, 73
  TRICARE, 10–11, 126
Federal Sentencing Guidelines, 58
Fee schedule, 116
Fee-for-service plans
  advantage plans, 8
  defined, 5, 12–13, 116
  discounted, 12, 114
  Medicaid and, 5
  Medicare Part A, 2, 5
  Medicare Part B, 2, 5
  Medigap and, 5
  point-of-service plans and, 15
  PPOs and, 15
  timely filing, 79
FEHB (Federal Employees Health Benefits Program)
  BCBS and, 20
  defined, 2, 116
Filing claims, 78–81, 91
Fiscal agent, 3–4
Fiscal intermediary, 116
Flexible Savings Account (FSA), 16
Food and Drug Administration, 3
For-profit insurance. *See* Commercial for-profit insurance
Fraud
  defined, 77, 116
  in documentation process, 77
  OIG compliance guidelines and, 59
Frustration, managing, 27–28
FSA (Flexible Savings Account), 16–17, 93

G

GA modifier, 6
Gatekeeper, 15, 116
Geographic practice cost indices (GPCIs), 47
Global billing, 116
Global period, 116
Global surgical package

billing requirements, 103–4
defined, 103, 116
modifiers, 104–5
Government insurance. *See also* Rules
    and regulations
    about, 1–2
    Medicaid, 8–10, 119–20
    Medicare, 2–8, 120
    TRICARE, 10–11, 126
GPCIs (geographic practice cost indices),
    47–48
Gross charges, 116
Group health plans
    defined, 116
    Medicare and, 56
    as primary payer, 7
    scenario, 96
Guarantee issue, 116–17

H

HCFA (Health Care Financing Adminis-
    tration), 111
HCPCS (Healthcare Common Procedure
    Coding System)
    CCI code pairs, 49–51
    defined, 117
    HIPAA regulations, 60
    J-codes, 119
Health Care Financing Administration
    (HCFA), 111
Health care insurance
    commercial for-profit insurance, 11–19
    fundamental elements, 14
    government insurance, 1–11
    non-governmental not-for-profit
        insurance, 19–20
Health Insurance Portability and Ac-
    countability Act. *See* HIPAA
    (Health Insurance Portability and
    Accountability Act)
Health Maintenance Organization. *See*
    HMO (Health Maintenance Orga-
    nization)
Health plans, 117
Health Reimbursement Account (HRA),
    16–17, 117
Health Saving Account (HSA), 16–17,
    117–18
Healthcare Common Procedure Coding
    System. *See* HCPCS (Healthcare
    Common Procedure Coding System)
HHS (Department of Health and Human
    Services)
    CMS, 111

defined, 113
    OIG division, 25, 122
HIPAA (Health Insurance Portability and
    Accountability Act)
    claims format, 59–60
    on clearinghouses, 78
    CPT codes, 46
    defined, 112, 117
    EDI provision, 114
    guarantee issue, 116–17
    MIP and, 77
    NPI mandate, 7, 121
    PHI protection, 124
    on pre-existing conditions, 123
    on professional courtesy, 124
    role of, 57–58
    X12 837 standard, 127
HIPAA Privacy Rule, 57–58, 78
History of Present Illness (HPI), 75
HMO (Health Maintenance Organization)
    advantage plans and, 3, 8
    defined, 15, 117
    managed care and, 12, 15, 119–20
Hospital encounters, 118
Hospitalists, 118
HPI (History of Present Illness), 75
HRA (Health Reimbursement Account),
    16–17, 117
HSA (Health Saving Account), 16–17,
    117–18

I

ICD-9 codes
    defined, 46, 113, 118
    documentation requirements, 75
    HIPAA regulations, 60
    plan for correct coding, 46–47
Incident to services, 118
Indemnity insurance, 118
Independence Practice Association/
    Organization (IPA/IPO), 118
Information overload, 26–27
Information processing
    by medical insurance staff, 23–24
    in revenue cycle, 64–65
    scenario, 92–93
Informed Consent for Treatment, 54
Inquiry, 118
Insurance cards
    billing process and, 53
    information processing and, 23, 65
Insurance carriers
    contracting with, 63–64
    correspondence, 86

defined, 111, 118–19
managing frustration with, 27–28
physician credentialing, 70–74
Insurance payments, 14
Insurance verification, 54–57
Internet-only manual (IOM), 59
IOM (Internet-only manual), 59
IPA/IPO (Independence Practice Association/Organization), 118

J

JCAHO (Joint Commission on Accreditation of Healthcare Organizations), 119
J-codes, 119
Joint Commission, 119
Justice, Department of, 72–73

K

Kickback, 59, 119
Kimball, Justin, 19

L

LCD (Local Coverage Determination), 119
Liability insurance
Medicare and, 57
as primary payer, 7, 55
scenario, 101
Lifetime limit, 119
Lipsky, Michael, 21
Local Coverage Determination (LCD), 119
Local coverage policy, 119

M

MAC (Medicare Administrative Contractor)
defined, 4, 52, 120
Medicare appeals process, 84–85
Malpractice claims history, 73
Malpractice expense (RVUm), 48
Managed care plans
defined, 6, 13–15, 119
Medicare Part C, 3–4, 6
Managed competition, 2
Maximum allowable charge, 119
Medicaid
defined, 8–9, 119–20
eligibility groups, 9
eligibility time frame, 10
fee-for-service plans, 5
mandatory services, 10
scenario, 90
Medical decision making, 76

Medical Group Management Association (MGMA), 82, 87
Medical group practice, 120
Medical liability insurance, 73
Medical necessity, 59, 120
Medical office insurance staff
actions of, 36
attitudes of, 34–35
beliefs of, 35
characteristics of, 28–33
charge capture and, 65–66
demand for services, 22
documentation considerations, 74–75
EDI system and, 60
effective communication, 32–33
as emerging profession, 42–43
goal expectations, 22
influences in Medicare implementation, 40–42
information processing, 23–24
key challenges, 24–28
major tensions, 36–40
measuring performance, 22
Medicare claims processing, 4
non-voluntary clients, 22
perceptions of, 33–34
as persistent, 29–30
placing emphasis on experience, 31
resources available, 22
as responsible, 28–29
scenario, 101–2
as self-reliant, 30–31
as street-level bureaucrats, 21–23
Medical power of attorney, 120
Medical records
defined, 120
documentation requirements, 75
fraud and abuse, 77–78
Medical reviews, 120
Medically Unlikely Edits (MUEs), 51–52
Medicare
ABN information, 6
advantage plans, 3, 6, 8
appeal process, 84–85
beneficiary enrollment, 7–8
claims format, 59–60
claims processing, 3–4, 23, 54
CMS 1500 form, 54
defined, 2, 120
effective communication with, 33
EFT authorization, 60
influences in implementation, 40–42
insurance verification, 54–57

National Correct Coding Initiative Coding Policy Manual for Medicare Services, 49
non-participating providers, 6
participation in, 5
primary payers, 7
provider enrollment, 7
scenario, 92, 100–102
secondary payers, 7
site-of-service payment consideration, 5
tensions dealing with, 37–40
timely filing and, 79–80
website, 8
Medicare Administrative Contractor (MAC), 4, 52, 120
Medicare Advantage. *See* Medicare Part C
Medicare Appeals Court, 84–85
Medicare Claims Processing Manual, 59
Medicare Integrity Program (MIP), 77
Medicare Medical Savings Accounts, 8
Medicare Part A
    beneficiary enrollment, 7–8
    claims processing, 3–4
    coverage eligibility, 4
    defined, 2, 120
    fee-for-service plans, 2, 5
    payment requests, 6
    scenario, 97
Medicare Part B
    beneficiary enrollment, 8
    claims processing, 3–4
    coverage eligibility, 4
    defined, 2–3, 8, 120
    fee-for-service plans, 2, 5
    open enrollment period, 8
Medicare Part C
    coverage eligibility, 4
    defined, 3, 120
    managed care plans, 3–4, 6
Medicare Part D
    coverage eligibility, 4
    defined, 3, 120
Medicare Physician Fee Schedule (MPFS), 48, 120
Medicare Redetermination Notice (MRN), 85
Medicare Remittance Advice (RA), 120
Medicare Secondary Payer (MSP), 56
Medicare Summary Notice (MSN), 121
Medigap
    CMS 1500 form, 54
    defined, 121
    fee-for-service plans, 5

Medicare beneficiary enrollment, 8
    scenario, 97
MGMA (Medical Group Management Association), 82, 87
MIP (Medicare Integrity Program), 77
Modifier 22, 105
Modifier 24, 105
Modifier 25, 104–5
Modifier 51, 105
Modifier 52, 105
Modifier 54, 104–5
Modifier 55, 104–5
Modifier 57, 104–5
Modifier 58, 104–5
Modifier 59, 104–5
Modifier 78, 105
Modifier 79, 105
Modifiers
    ABN information, 6
    defined, 103–5, 121
MPFS (Medicare Physician Fee Schedule), 48, 120
MRN (Medicare Redetermination Notice), 85
MSN (Medicare Summary Notice), 121
MSP (Medicare Secondary Payer), 56
MUEs (Medically Unlikely Edits), 51–52
Multi-specialty practice, 121
Multi-tiered plan, 121
Mutual of Omaha, 3

N

National Correct Coding Initiative. *See* NCCI (National Correct Coding Initiative)
National Correct Coding Initiative Coding Policy Manual for Medicare Services, 49
National Coverage Determination (NCD), 119, 121
National payer identifier, 121
National Provider Identifier (NPI), 7, 121
National Technical Information Service (NTIS), 49, 52
NCCI (National Correct Coding Initiative)
    about, 7
    billing process and, 48–52
    defined, 112, 121
    mailing address, 52
NCD (National Coverage Determination), 119, 121
Network, 121
No-fault insurance
    Medicare and, 57
    as primary payer, 7, 55

Non-assigned claims, 5, 121
Non-facility (PE-nf)
    defined, 115, 122
    place of service codes, 107
Non-governmental not-for-profit insur-
        ance, 19–20
Non-participating providers
    defined, 122
    EOBs and, 70
    Medicare and, 6
Non-physician providers, 122
Not-for-profit insurance, 19–20
Notice of Exclusions of Medicare Ben-
        efits, 122
NP (nurse practitioner), 45
NPI (National Provider Identifier), 7, 121
NTIS (National Technical Information
        Service), 49, 52
Nurse practitioner (NP), 45

O

OCE (Outpatient Code Editor), 52
OCR (Office for Civil Rights), 57
Office for Civil Rights (OCR), 57
Office of Inspector General. *See* OIG
        (Office of Inspector General)
Offsets, 88, 122
OIG (Office of Inspector General)
    compliance guidelines, 58–59
    defined, 122
    responsibilities of, 25
Open access, 122
Open enrollment period, 8, 122
Out-of-network, 122
Out-of-pocket maximum, 122
Outpatient Code Editor (OCE), 52
Overpayment, 122

P

P4P (pay for performance), 123
PA (physician assistant), 45
Participating providers
    defined, 123
    EOBs and, 69–70
    Medicare participation, 5
Past, Family, Social History (PFSH), 75
Patient correspondence, 86
Patient identification, 53
Patient paperwork
    billing process and, 52–54
    insurance cards, 23, 53, 65
    patient identification, 53
    scenario, 92–93, 95–96
    signature on file, 53–54

Pay for performance (P4P), 123
Payer mix, 123
Payers
    defined, 123
    Medicare as, 7
    primary, 7
    secondary, 7
Payment posting, 81–82
PC (professional component), 124–25
PCP (primary care physician), 124
PE-f (facility), 107, 115
PE-nf (non-facility)
    defined, 115, 122
    place of service codes, 107
PFSH (Past, Family, Social History), 75
PHI (protected health information), 60,
        124
Physician assistant (PA), 45
Physician credentialing, 70–74
Physicians
    charge capture, 66, 98
    defined, 123
    Medicare claims processing, 4
    Medicare participation, 5
    RVUw, 48
    scenario, 98–100
Place of service codes, 107, 123
Point of service. *See* POS (point of service)
Portability, 123
POS (point of service)
    defined, 15–17, 119, 123
    managed care and, 12, 15
PPO (preferred provider organization)
    advantage plans and, 3, 8
    defined, 15, 119, 123
    managed care and, 12, 15
Practice expense (RVUpe), 48
Pre-certification, 123
Pre-existing condition, 123
Preferred provider organization. *See* PPO
        (preferred provider organization)
Premiums, 14
Prescription drug plans, 3–4
Pricer/repricer, 124
Primary care physician (PCP), 124
Primary insurance
    determining, 23, 54
    Medicare as, 7
Prior authorization, 123–24
Procedures
    code sets on, 60
    CPT codes for, 45
    RBRVS system, 47
Professional component (PC), 124–25

Professional courtesy, 124
Protected health information (PHI), 60, 124
Providers
  defined, 124
  enrollment in Medicare program, 7
  non-participating, 6, 70, 122
  non-physician, 122
  participating, 5, 69–70, 123

Q

QIC (qualified independent contractor), 85
Qualified independent contractor (QIC), 85

R

Railroad Retirement Board (RRB), 113
RBRVS (Resource-Based Relative Value Scale)
  defined, 47, 125
  factors for calculating fees, 47–48
  GF component, 47–48
  GPCI component, 47–48
  RVU component, 47–48
Re-aged accounts receivable, 124
Record retention, 124–25
Recoupment, 88, 125
Regulations. See Rules and regulations
Reimbursement
  as billing process goal, 45
  information processing and, 23
Relative value unit. See RVU (relative value unit)
Release-of-information forms, 54
Remittance advice, 125
Reopening claims, 85
Resource-Based Relative Value Scale. See RBRVS (Resource-Based Relative Value Scale)
Revenue cycle
  account follow-up, 82–85
  charge capture, 65–66
  charge entry, 66
  coding in, 74–76
  collections and, 87–88
  contract negotiations, 63–64
  correspondence in, 86–87
  documentation in, 74–76
  elements, 63–68
  EOB in, 68–70
  filing claims, 78–81
  fraud and abuse in, 77–78
  generating claims, 66–67

information collection, 64–65
payment posting, 81–82
physician credentialing, 70–74
submitting claims, 66–67
working claims, 67–68
Review of Systems (ROS), 75
ROS (Review of Systems), 75
RRB (Railroad Retirement Board), 4, 113
Rules and regulations
  adhering to, 24–26
  claims format, 59–60, 66–67
  CMS and, 45
  HIPAA Privacy Rule, 57–58, 78
  information overload, 26–27
  insurance verification, 54–57
  OIG compliance guidelines, 58–59
RVU (relative value unit)
  components of, 48
  defined, 47, 115, 125
  modifiers, 103–5, 121
  place of service codes, 107
RVUm (malpractice expense), 48
RVUpe (practice expense), 48
RVUw (work), 48, 51

S

Same-day surgery center, 110
Secondary insurance
  determining, 23, 54
  Medicare as, 7
Self-insurance, 16, 125
Self-pay, 125
Self-referral, 59
Service delivery, 41–42
SGR (sustainable growth rate), 47
Signature on file (patient), 53–54, 95–96
Site-of-service payment consideration, 5
Skilled nursing facility (SNF), 107
SNF (skilled nursing facility), 107
Social Security Act
  defined, 125
  Medicare provisions, 2, 120
Social Security Administration, 7
SSI (Supplemental Security Income), 9
Street-level bureaucrats, 21–23
Subscribers, 125
Supplemental Medical Insurance. See Medicare Part B
Supplemental Security Income (SSI), 9
Sustainable growth rate (SGR), 47

T

TC (technical component), 124–25
Third-party administrator (TPA), 19, 125

Third-party payer, 126
Timely filing, 79–80, 126
TPA (third-party administrator), 19, 125
Transaction and Code Sets Standards, 60
Transactions, 60
TRICARE
    defined, 10–11, 126
    as primary payer, 7, 56

U

UCR (Usual, Customary, Reasonable)
        charges, 126
Unbundling services, 126
Underpayment, 126
Unique physician identifier number
        (UPIN), 121
Unit of service (UOS), 51–52
Universal Credentialing Data Source, 113
Universal Provider Datasource, 74
Unprocessable claim, 126
UOS (unit of service), 51–52
UPIN (unique physician identifier
        number), 121
Usual, Customary, Reasonable (UCR)
        charges, 126

Utilization, 126
Utilization review, 126

V

Vendors, 126
Veterans Affairs, Department of, 7

W

Weick, Karl, 26
Whistle-blowers, 126
Work (RVUw), 48, 51
Worker's compensation
    defined, 18, 126–27
    Medicare and, 57
    as primary payer, 7, 55
Workers' Compensation Board, 18
Working claims. *See* Accounts receivable
WPS (Wisconsin Physicians Services)
        Insurance Corporation, 3

X

X12 837 standard, 127